The Confidence Formula:
May Cause: Lower Self-Doubt, Higher Self-Esteem, and Comfort In Your Own Skin

By Patrick King

Social Interaction and Conversation Coach at
www.PatrickKingConsulting.com

4

Table of Contents

Chapter 1. The Ripple Effect of Confidence

There was a time in my life when I was deeply uncomfortable placing my order at McDonald's. However, it wasn't because I had inner turmoil about the massive load of saturated fat I was about to put into my body. It was because I had to *speak to someone* to do it. Sounds crazy, huh? If you're reading this book, though, I'm guessing it sounds a little too familiar . . .

I remember one particular instance at an Applebee's. The waitress had come around to my side of the table to take my order, but I wasn't quite ready so I tried to stall her by asking her what she recommended.

I could sense her eyes burning a hole through my menu, the rest of the table staring at me and wishing I hadn't come, and the cooks in the back covertly planning to spit in my food. I started sweating all over and my ears became so hot I thought they were going to melt right off my head. I had made such a huge mistake, and now deserved to be outcast from the group.

I felt rushed and latched on to the first menu item my eyes landed on. When the food came, I ate it as quickly as possible, left some money on the table, and, to my friends' protests, made up an excuse about having to go home. At home, I stewed over it for eons—after all, it was the single most embarrassing and awful disaster that had ever happened, right?

Of course, to everyone else, their friend was just asking the waitress for her recommendation, and to the waitress, a customer was having a difficult time deciding what to order. That's it. These might have been your thoughts as well; that I was making incredible leaps to conclusions that were blown out of proportion. But at no point did I truly think I was acting irrationally. I felt I had made such a blunder that I deserved to be cast out from civilized society. Seriously.

That's the role of confidence in our lives, and I'm speaking as someone who's been in your shoes and knows how it feels. I know how crippling and fear-driven it is, and how it can prevent you from living life the way you want to. Little by little over the years, I conquered my fears of ordering food at restaurants, and graduated to becoming comfortable with public speaking and meeting new people. I've come a long way from that day in Applebee's.

Confidence may not be a cure-all, but because it can be so deeply rooted within people for so long, it causes us anxiety in ways we may not realize.

There's a poetic saying proposing when a butterfly flaps its wings in Brazil, it causes a tsunami in Japan. What does that mean? No matter how small an action, there will always be a consequence. We may not perceive it, and it may barely be felt, but there is always some sort of reaction for each action.

A butterfly might displace only a single breath's worth of air, but as it travels, that tiny flutter of air can easily snowball and aggregate into a monstrous tsunami. The aftereffects of seemingly small actions are often hidden, unintended, or flat-out ignored.

This is the ripple effect, and though it's easier to observe in other situations, it is imperative to understand in the context of confidence. Lack of belief and confidence in yourself has wide-ranging consequences you may not even be aware of, and they affect every corner of your life. The smallest absence of confidence can grow and compound in a way that makes you unable to recognize yourself in the mirror.

If affects your entire outlook on life, and not

just when you're at a networking event or birthday party. It's more than something keeping you from going to a party, or from talking to a stranger. It's the story you've told about yourself since you were young, and it influences all your patterns of thought. And these seemingly flimsy thoughts and feelings have a funny way of becoming a self-fulfilling prophecy. They may start out tiny and imperceptible, but in a real way, can eventually manifest concretely in the choices we make, the choices we don't . . . and the people we become.

The best way to understand the impact of low confidence is to contrast the beliefs it can cause with the beliefs of people who have high confidence. By taking a good hard look at what it's like *not* to be crippled by low-confidence and anxiety, we can get a good idea of where to start on our own journey to better self-esteem. The first thing to do, probably, is to really believe that you, too, can be one of those people.

People who possess high self-esteem and confidence take almost all of the following for granted, and why wouldn't they? Shouldn't you? It might seem like they are low, basic expectations, but that's where the separation is found. These are the miniscule butterfly wing flaps that ultimately create tsunamis!

Socially confident people expect to be accepted. When they meet strangers, they *expect* to make a good impression and don't get entangled in or stymied by fears they will be negatively perceived by others. They take for granted that people will react positively to them. They never approach situations thinking, "What if they don't like me?" Instead, they think, "I hope I like them."

They have the same adrenaline coursing through their veins when they meet strangers, but it manifests as excitement, whereas for others it will manifest as anxiety. Rather than fear, they have a relaxed interest or curiosity. This turns the prospect of anything new into an opportunity for gain rather than a minefield to be careful in or avoid completely.

Socially confident people evaluate themselves positively. This is partially due to the way they talk to themselves, and partially due to their positive self-perception. What do these mean? Socially confident people are encouraging, positive, and accepting of themselves. They give themselves leeway not to be perfect and don't beat themselves up too harshly when they are not.

They also rate their social abilities according to a positive baseline. If they do well, that's par for the course. They expected that. If they do poorly, it's an occasional exception that they can learn from. They don't allow themselves to be affected by singular incidents they know don't represent their abilities. They think highly of themselves in a healthy manner and aren't afraid of constant judgment.

Socially confident people can deal with criticism. Criticism doesn't crumble them. This is related to the previous point. Confident people learn to compartmentalize and separate criticism and recognize its actual purpose; they do not take it personally in an emotional way or assume that criticism is an attack—at least as much as humanly possible.

Their identity doesn't ebb and flow because of a single errant comment. It doesn't cause them to question their entire being or worth. They know they have worth even if they have faltered in a single area. They are not afraid that criticism will confirm a harsh truth about themselves they've been trying to avoid. In fact, they seek criticism because they know they need it to improve and will be better off for it.

Socially confident people feel comfortable around superiors. Define superior however you want—someone who is better looking, more athletic, further up in the office hierarchy, or more outgoing and charming. Socially confident people feel comfortable because they don't feel threatened, or that their flaws and vulnerabilities will be highlighted by the other person's qualities. They don't have the specters of constant self-consciousness and rejection hanging over them.

They can celebrate the talents and triumphs of others because they know that others' accomplishments do not diminish (and should not discourage) their own. They know the world doesn't run on an invisible currency that requires others to lose in order for them to win. In fact, they look forward to spending time with "superiors" because they know that's the key to learning and bettering themselves, as opposed to revealing flaws. They might feel competitive, but not subordinated. In another way, they understand that in the grand scheme, people are people, and even if someone is "better" than them in one way, they're likely "worse" in another way.

Are these simple aspects of interacting with others a given in *your* mind? In contrast, how do people who *lack* confidence approach the world?

People without confidence expect rejection. Before they even step into a situation, in the back of their minds, they are already anticipating failure. It's like they've prejudged and pre-condemned themselves and are just waiting for reality to catch up with their assessment. They're looking for cues that people are disinterested or bored with them. They think twice before speaking and effectively censor themselves. They basically have a bad reputation with themselves.

They are already thinking they will make fools of themselves, so they expect the worst-case scenario. This shows in their facial expressions and body language, and does indeed cause people to react poorly to them. They cause their worst-case scenario to come true because they never allow themselves to be vulnerable or open to others.

When you expect rejection, you feel helpless, as if nothing you can possibly do will make a difference. Picture how a person's posture changes when they are expecting to be hit. Now, imagine the psychological equivalent. Do you cringe and cower internally because on some level, you're always expecting some kind of blow? Even worse, if you feel like there's not much you can do to defend yourself, you'll naturally avoid the perceived threat. People start seeming like more trouble than they're worth. Following that logic, why would you leave your home to try at all? You'd feel hopeless and stay as still as possible to avoid any negativity.

People without confidence evaluate themselves negatively. In stark contrast to those who are socially confident, unconfident people evaluate themselves from a baseline of negativity. They just don't believe in themselves or their abilities. If they perform well, they view it as an isolated anomaly. They shock themselves and don't believe it will last. They expect the worst and often get it because of this expectation. There is no opportunity, only room to trip and fail; a rope to hang themselves with.

People without confidence crumble under criticism. Criticism is a nightmare for the unconfident. On the surface they might put up a fight and appear viciously defensive, but deep down, they feel the criticism is warranted and deserved. All of their worst fears are continually confirmed, even if the criticism was benign or unrelated.

Their self-perception already hangs by a thread, so any small criticism can sever that thread and plunge them into an abyss of negativity. It's a crack in their armor that is representative of their entire value as a human being. Whatever shortcoming they've been attempting to conceal will be exposed by criticism. And then they will have to face the harsh reality of their failings.

Unconfident people will steer clear of the

spotlight and take action as a way of avoiding negative feedback that might confirm their worst fears.

People without confidence are highly uncomfortable around superiors. Unconfident people are threatened by those they view as superiors. This is fueled in equal parts by jealousy, lack of confidence, and viewing social situations as zero-sum games—there can only be one winner, so everyone else has to be a loser (including them).

They feel swept up in a tornado when someone who is socially superior comes by. Not only do those with low confidence feel constantly judged, superiors are a reminder of what they feel they can never attain or be. Furthermore, they compare themselves to their superiors in a way that emphasizes all their own shortcomings. Cue the stereotype of the short man who buys an enormous truck to feel less inadequate.

A lack of confidence can run deep. What might appear to be a relatively small shortcoming can ultimately determine how one lives their life. Because you are driven by fear, a line is drawn in the sand as to where you can go, how far you can go, and what is worth your effort. As time goes on, this self-created circle of capability, competency, and confidence begins to collapse and shrink. Eventually, you'll feel trapped.

If you stay where you are, you're standing in a sealed room that is quickly filling to the top with water. You can't stay there. You cannot keep running away from your social anxiety and fears. You need to act. If you don't change, nothing will.

You will have imprisoned yourself behind invisible bars. You can do whatever you want, but you choose not to because of those invisible walls—walls that were *not* created by people who have it out for you. There are no evil ogres keeping you down. Just you.

This is the ripple effect. You encounter people in the office, in your neighborhood, and even when you shop for groceries or get a cup of coffee. These things happen every day. How will you choose to handle yourself? You may think you're not missing out on much, but if you add and compound these interactions, your days will blur together with nothingness. A series of small avoidances and imaginary confirmations grow larger and larger until the tsunami hits you and you're left paralyzed.

The anxiety and accompanying discomfort you feel makes you engage in anti-social behavior. As a result, you receive negative or lukewarm feedback. You internalize this feedback and create an even more meek and uncomfortable version of yourself. Anxiety builds and you sink deeper into the quicksand. You deeply fear judgment, failure, rejection, and being thought of as stupid. Just like that, with the snap of a finger, you feel that you can be doomed.

Confidence can make you feel like the king of the world, but it's not as easy as simply making the choice. For one thing, basic human psychology is against your side.

Low Confidence Characteristics

Everybody who lacks confidence experiences their trepidation in different ways. Some are obvious; others are less noticeable. And most, of course, are automatic to the point where the social phobic doesn't even realize they're happening. These behaviors and thought processes might be any of the following:

They process external events and social cues in a negative way. The social phobic doesn't differentiate between neutral and negative reactions; to them, any reply that's not explicitly positive is disapproval to some degree. If someone responds in an ambiguous way, the social phobic interprets it as a negative. And if somebody offers even the mildest, most well-intentioned criticism, they'll cast it as a complete disaster.

For example, if social phobic Bridget is talking to her friend Greta about a problem in her relationship with her boyfriend, Stuart, and Greta periodically looks away or doesn't necessarily show intense interest, Bridget might interpret that as a rejection from Greta. And if Greta gently suggests that Bridget look at the problem from another point of view, Bridget might interpret that as treason. She might even accuse Greta of taking Stuart's side.

They over-focus on themselves when anxious. The social phobic has a hard time fitting in with the flow of a social event because they're unable to tone down their self-awareness. This can make them seem aloof or distracted— which only serves to confirm their own low self-opinion. For example, if a social phobic is overly conscious of his appearance at a cocktail party, he might constantly check his reflection in mirrors, windows, or wine glasses. The constant monitoring would impact whatever socializing he went to the party for in the first place.

They distort their self-image in fearful situations. When they're in a stressful environment, the social phobic tends to see themselves from an observer's standpoint—and what they see is usually a twisted version of themselves. This self-image is frequently linked to bitter memories of the past, including ones where they were bullied, shamed, or reprimanded.

The information a social phobic retains from those memories is often exaggerated; for example, they'll imagine they looked like they were having a nervous breakdown in front of a crowd—when in reality, they showed no outward symptoms of a panic attack at all. They might have even looked completely stoic to everyone in the room. But in their mind's eye, they were cracking like an egg and everyone knew it.

Safety behaviors reinforce their negativity—and taints how others perceive them. The social phobic's reliance and emphasis on staying secure overshadows the reality of the situation they're experiencing. They maintain their negative perceptions and refuse to believe evidence that disproves them. Over-reliance on their safety behaviors in public can make a social phobic appear distant, aloof, or unsympathetic to others. This is, of course, an accidental upshot of their safety behaviors: it leaves them more open to the criticism and rejection those behaviors are supposed to prevent.

For example, a man with zero self-esteem and an inferiority complex about his likability might constantly gossip about other people to reinforce his feelings of superiority—but as a result, everyone hates being around him and his plan backfires.

They dread upcoming social situations and brood on the negatives afterward. The person with low confidence develops an adverse anticipation of approaching events. They recall past events that didn't end well. They prepare their safety behaviors for the next event and might even try to plan an escape route. For example, a businessperson might be terrified of a company cocktail mixer because they remember a past get-together where they had too much to drink and think they acted foolishly.

You're probably noticing a bit of a theme with all these characteristics. People with low confidence are, to use a clichéd expression, their own worst enemy. For people who lack self-esteem, the world can seem like one big problem and they themselves are a big problem, too. In a way, people with low confidence really *do* have a serious problem— just not the one they think they have! Their problem is not that they are inferior, but that they are constantly telling themselves a story of their own inferiority—it's a big difference!

These common experiences plague the psyche of the socially anxious and can accumulate mentally to the extent where there doesn't seem to be any way to repair them. But there is: through trying to understand what's really fueling their social phobia. Sometimes the answer is buried deep in their back history and they have to drag it out. Sometimes it's right there on the surface, waiting for us to be courageous enough to act.

Am I Unconfident—or Do I Have Anxiety?

I have a friend who is what others would consider a social butterfly. She's popular, likable, and an excellent communicator. You would never know it, but she's also deeply unconfident. In my friend's case, she's a bit like an extrovert who nevertheless has a low opinion of her own self-worth. When you get to know her, you realize that despite appearances, she actually has a shockingly low self-esteem.

My friend is not a common case, however. In my experience, low self-esteem, lack of confidence, and social anxiety all tend to go hand in hand. Because we think so little of ourselves, we process events with a negative bias and tend to hyper focus on ourselves in an anxious, distorted way. And naturally, that's going to manifest when we engage with other people. Soon, it can start to seem like the problem is that we're shy, introverted, withdrawn, reserved, or depressed, when actually, the problem is that we simply lack any faith in our own ability to take part in the social world.

What I mean is that what looks like social anxiety on the surface may be nothing more than lack of confidence. If you can combat these low feelings of self-worth, you may be surprised to find that you actually *enjoy* other people and are not shy or reserved at all. In the chapters that follow, we'll be talking about social anxiety, low self-esteem, and lack of confidence interchangeably. They're not the same thing, but they do form a cluster around the same patterns of negative bias, anxiety, thought distortion, and discomfort with others. Social anxiety can be a symptom of lack of confidence, but it's also a cause and reinforcer of these patterns of thinking and behavior.

The Spotlight Effect

Poor self-confidence is driven by the gripping fear that one's action and behaviors will be judged unfavorably by others. We fear that we are bad or wrong or inferior, and the social anxiety element enters the picture when we worry that others will perceive this in us too and judge us for it. But are they really watching as closely as you think they are? Are they really all laughing internally at your smallest mistakes and blunders? You might just be feeling the burden of the spotlight effect.

The spotlight effect is a psychological phenomenon when our minds exaggerate just how much other people are paying attention to us. We're terrified that everyone in the room is watching everything we do and listening to everything we say and are judging us accordingly. Perhaps because we ourselves are so intently focused on our own experience, we imagine that everyone else is as absorbed in our exploits—and judging them as mercilessly.

In reality, though, nobody's really paying that much attention. If you doubt this, you can do a quick thought experiment. Try to imagine the last social event or conversation you were part of, and ask yourself whether you were intently watching and analyzing other people. Did any one person have a spotlight on them? Probably not.

Of course, the sensation that we are "on the spot" and being observed is doubly damaging when you are already suffering from low confidence. The feeling that everyone is watching, in addition to detrimental beliefs about yourself, can be downright paralyzing.

The term "spotlight effect" was partially coined by psychologist Thomas Gilovich, who ran a couple of amusing studies on the subject in the 1990s. In the first, Gilovich's team assembled a group of students in a room and randomly selected one. That student was asked to wear a T-shirt that featured pop singer Barry Manilow on the front. (For those of you who don't have access to your grandparents' record collection, Manilow was considered about as uncool as a musician could be in the nineties, fairly or not.)

After a little while in which the student was forced to mix with others and accept his new reality as a Manilow fan, researchers asked him to estimate how many of their other fellow students *he* thought recognized the portrait on their T-shirt. The student estimated that half of them did. The actual figure was closer to twenty-five percent.

Gilovich did a second study with different students using the exact same process, with one big exception: after being in the room with the others, the Manilow student was put in a separate room by themselves for fifteen minutes before giving their estimate. This gave the student additional time to become accustomed to having Barry Manilow's face on their shirt. In this trial, the student's estimate was more on target. They said they expected about twenty-five percent of the other students recognized Manilow's portrait.

The findings implied that one's personal experience heavily influences how they perceive the judgments of others. When the student was initially put in the uncomfortable bind of wearing a Barry Manilow shirt and then thrust into the wild, he assumed that most people were easily able to identify the singer, and possibly casting a private verdict on his musical taste and hipness as well.

But after a little while in which he adjusted to having a picture of the number one pop crooner of the seventies emblazoned upon his chest, his assessment of who was actually paying attention was much more accurate. Even when we behave in unusual or potentially embarrassing ways, we tend to overestimate how much people are noticing or judging us. The reality is, we're just not that interesting or important—and that's a good thing. As an unconfident person, you may be walking around with a very negative bias toward yourself, when the truth is that, well, most people don't really care!

It's easy to understand why the spotlight effect can be so afflicting. We live in our own bodies and minds twenty-four hours a day. It's natural for us to be preoccupied with our own characteristics, traits and past experiences. After all, *we* are. This is the same thing that causes us to lack empathy or sympathy for others - because we are simply thinking *me* all the time. In turn, it can be difficult for us to understand and admit that other people aren't as intensely concentrated on our actions. This kind of circumstance is called "anchoring and adjustment": We're so fixed on our own selves and experience that we can't precisely judge how much—or more accurately, how little— other people are really watching us.

After one lives in new skin for a reasonable amount of time, their self-awareness gradually decreases and the spotlight effect fades. Knowing that you're far more off the hook than you originally thought will benefit your confidence. And don't worry, I won't tell anyone how much you love "Copacabana."

Next time you're out in public, conduct a little experiment to provide evidence to yourself that people aren't solely focused on judging you. Just take a few minutes to stare at someone in public. Make sure they don't see you, of course. Just look at them and try to notice what they are preoccupied with. Most likely, they aren't paying the slightest bit of attention to anyone besides themselves. Now, look at someone else. Are they looking around as you are and judging everyone in their vicinity? No, they probably are not.

Now, do something small you think would warrant a reaction if they were really watching you covertly. Something like taking off your shoe and smelling it, stretching obnoxiously, or making weird shapes with your face and mouth. Are they staring at you, slack-jawed, ready to gather a mob for ridicule? There's no spotlight besides the one you create in your mind.

Feelings Versus Automatic Thoughts

The spotlight effect is based on our expectations of other people reacting to our actions, and the feeling of terror about how those reactions will make us feel.

Humans tend to believe that their emotions are directly caused by other people or external events: "My in-laws make me anxious," "That movie made me upset," "That spa session calmed me down." The implication is that we don't have cognitive input on what affects us—things happen, or people say things, and they flick certain triggers, resulting in a negative or positive emotion. Indeed, the way we feel fear and other negative feelings can often appear to be automatic, or at least not up for debate.

Event occurs, feelings ensue. Except that that's not the whole story.

In reality, there's an intermediary step—number two in this sequence:

1. We experience an event.

2. *We perceive what the event means to us.*

3. We have a feeling about the event.

What really fuels our feelings are our seemingly automatic *perceptions* of situations and other people. We don't recognize these thoughts when they happen because they're extremely quick. So it *seems* like our feelings are directly fed by the events we experience. But we're actually filtering those feelings through our thoughts—even though they happen so fast we don't notice them.

Events themselves are neutral, but it's that critical second step that imbues them with meaning and determines what the final step, our thoughts and feelings, will be. It's up to you to make sure step two isn't working against you.

For example, let's say you're speaking with a casual acquaintance. You're talking about an experience at work with a new colleague you respect. You speak about him in fairly glowing terms. Your casual acquaintance smiles slightly and reveals that she knows your colleague well, because he's an ex. They broke up a year ago and haven't spoken since. You say you're sorry, that you didn't know. She waves her hand and says it's okay, no harm done.

If you perceive the conversation to be normal and commonplace, then you were just talking with someone you didn't know had a connection to your new colleague. You were completely innocent, discovered a funny coincidence, she said it was okay, and the world continued to rotate around a flaming ball of fire. But you could have an alternate reaction based on a negative self-perception and what others think of you:

- "Gosh, my oversharing with people can backfire. I must look so foolish."

- "It doesn't matter if it was an innocent mistake on my part—she must have thought I was heartless or unthinking."

- "Wow, I should have known. She'll probably hate me forever. Goodbye, friendship."

None of these ideas are actually a natural part of the situation itself. They're interpretations. Each of these emotive responses demonstrate how skewed your internal dialogue can become simply because you allow your perceptions to color an external event. It seems like a two-step process, but in reality, that middle step is so quick, it's basically unconscious. You may do it so quickly and effortlessly that you genuinely believe you are just perceiving reality rather than an *interpretation* or story about that reality. And then, you might be tempted to say things like, "She thinks I'm insensitive," placing the source of the emotion at her feet rather than seeing where it really comes from—you.

In most cases, automatic thoughts aren't particularly beneficial to us—especially when we're trying to build confidence. A negative automatic thought could lead to misunderstanding a situation and exaggerating the chances of a negative interaction or event.

If you see *your* ex in a bar when you're out with your friends, you might perceive it as a dangerous situation because you think you'll be uncomfortable or hostile. That's the negative automatic thought. But it could turn out just fine—maybe your ex is about to leave, they just won't approach you, or they'll respect your space. Or perhaps they'll be *nice*. This all depends on the state of your breakup, but it also depends on how you perceive the situation.

It's therefore very important to distinguish between thoughts and feelings. They aren't the same experience. Feelings are the *product* of thoughts. You could say, "I think I'm angry," but you only *feel* angry. What you're really thinking is, "Nobody in my office is lifting a finger to help me," or, "My kid is trying to push my boundaries," or, "This jerk is tailing me too closely."

When you come upon a certain situation and have some time to act upon it, it's a great idea to step back and consider several different thoughts could arise from it. With a lack of confidence, you are usually choosing the thought that is cruelest to yourself. You can learn to intercept yourself in the process of walking down a dark path, and we will cover that in the next chapter in greater detail. At the very least, turn a two-step process into three steps and realize that just because an external event occurs, you are not obligated to feel a certain way about it.

Blame the Amygdala

One of the biggest reasons our thoughts are so automatic is the bit of grey matter lodged between the two brain hemispheres: the amygdala.

The amygdala—a tiny, bean-shaped mass in the middle of the brain—is the source of much of our lack of confidence. It actually handles most of our various emotional responses, but it really kicks into high gear with the fight-or-flight response. Studies have shown that a highly active amygdala is more likely to trigger fright, dismay, uncertainty, and terror. In other words, when the amygdala gets even a whiff of something fearful or anxious, our reactions are no longer entirely conscious.

When threatened, the amygdala's response overrides the neocortex, which is associated with the logical and reasonable functions of the brain. The amygdala, as scientist Daniel Goleman explains, "hijacks" our response, whips it past the usually clear-thinking neocortex, and heads straight to the thalamus that's in charge of interpreting sensory input. Because the whole "think this through" process of the neocortex is completely ignored, when we feel fear, we perceive that it's coming from a very deep part of the mind that nobody can see and therefore fix.

The alarm sounds, and all our socially anxious behaviors snap to attention, all our rational responses go out the window, and fear rules the day. Our emotions go haywire, and we become pumped full of adrenaline.

Lack of self-confidence is, at least to the brain, a form of plain old fear. Every creature on earth has the ability to move toward something or away from it, to proceed with curiosity or even aggression, or to shrink back in the anticipation of being attacked. When we have low self-confidence, we have no faith in ourselves. We shrink back. We do not feel up to the task of living or the challenges set before us. Basically, we see the threat or situation ahead of us, and we judge ourselves as inadequate compared to it. This is not that different from a small animal fleeing in terror from a bigger animal.

The thing is, your estimation of being a "small" animal may be completely wrong. That doesn't mean, however, that your neurochemistry isn't participating as if the outside world is a genuine threat. So, if you have a negative bias, cognitive distortions, and deep core beliefs about your own inferiority, your amygdala registers it all and responds accordingly. Furthermore, the response completely bypasses the more rational, higher order parts of your cognition. You can *say*, "This emotion doesn't make sense," but it doesn't matter—on a primal level, you are still feeling that fear and apprehension, that sense that you are weak, less than, or inferior.

What this all boils down to is this: we can't cure our feelings of low self-esteem through rational thought or logic alone. It's great to *have* a set of reasonable and strong beliefs, and it certainly doesn't hurt. But if the amygdala goes on one of its little tirades, rationality might not be enough for the brain to fix itself. But we can *try* to reprogram our belief systems to where the amygdala doesn't have quite as much effect on our confidence.

In the chapters that follow, we'll be looking at different ways to work with or work around these primal, inbuilt biases and tendencies of our brains. In reality, low confidence and poor self-esteem are whole-body phenomena. When we feel bad about our worth as human beings, every part of us is involved, from our brain physiology and neurochemistry, to our thoughts and inner self-talk, to our everyday behaviors and choices, to the way we engage with others.

This is far less bleak than it seems, though. We can and should make changes to the way we think, feel, and behave, and this is far more within our control than it might first appear. There is one thing in particular that we can do to try to stem the tide of negativity from crashing over us, and we'll explore this more in the next section.

Your Confidence Resume

Take inventory—what does that mean?

In a grocery store, taking inventory is when you look at what you have in the store and try to account for everything. The purpose is to know what is currently in stock, what is needed, and if there are any trends worth pursuing.

Take inventory of your strengths and weaknesses, and you can accomplish the same three goals. You will be able to understand yourself as you currently are, see what shortcomings you have—if any—and examine if your inventory has any hidden data or trends.

In a more concrete sense, go through the exercise of taking a piece of paper, folding it in half, and writing your strengths you have on one side, and weaknesses on the other side. Don't think too hard about it or overanalyze what you're putting down—the longer you dawdle, the less chance you have of being honest! Write anything that comes to mind and stop after just a couple minutes. You probably won't need a long time to do this, as you probably have a few things in mind already.

How did the lists turn out? I'm betting the weakness side of the list was where you focused most of your attention, and the weakness side was at least one and half times longer than the strength side.

Why could I predict this? Because when people seeking confidence try to come up with strengths or anything else positive about themselves, it's incredibly difficult for them to do it objectively. The list on the positive side almost always turns out pitifully short to the point of inaccuracy and being misleading. If their best friend read only their lists of strengths and weaknesses, they might not even recognize that person from the description. So, this exercise is not one to help you conduct an inventory of your strengths and weaknesses, but rather get a good snapshot of your current mindset, core beliefs, and negative biases.

People lacking confidence are typically far too hard on themselves and have a skewed perception of their abilities. They have an almost impossible time in recognizing what they are actually good at and bad at because everything is fraught with negative emotion. If they excel at something, it feels like an anomaly or luck, so they discount it, forget it, or explain it away as somehow actually a bad thing. If they fail at something, it lines up with their expectations, so they hold on to it and amplify it, recalling first when they think of who they are and what they've done. In many cases, these weaknesses are purely imagined in the first place, and the strengths marginalized or justified away.

This laundry list of weaknesses is more a reflection of fear and past bad experiences rather than of reality. It turns out that many of our perceived weaknesses aren't weaknesses at all; they're just something we may have failed in *once* or don't have good memories of. Or, if they're genuinely weaknesses and flaws in our character, we inevitably blow them out of proportion and make them much worse than they really are. In any case, hopefully this exercise has helped you gain a little insight into how you perceive yourself—lacking in ability and talent, getting by on luck. On balance, kind of a bad person. This might be the first time you've put these feelings into words.

Now you are going to do this exercise again, but here's the catch: this time, you are going to focus on your *actual* strengths and weaknesses.

A strength is defined as something you are better than many of your friends at, or something you are objectively above average at. A weakness is defined in a similar way: something you are worse than many of your friends at, or something you are objectively below average at.

This time, as you write, try to imagine you are a friend or acquaintance who is writing the list. Think of all the compliments you've ever received, and how other people appraise you. What evidence do you actually have of either good or bad traits? If the answer is "not much," then leave it off. For example, saying something stupid once when you were ten years old doesn't mean you're unintelligent.

The lists should be just about even in length—for every weakness, list a strength to make sure that you are accurately describing yourself. If you decide to get a head start by importing some strengths and weaknesses from the first list—what does and doesn't make the cut? In other words, what weaknesses are you omitting and why? For greater objectivity, have a friend help edit your lists. Often, people will refuse to fill the list out objectively despite being given the new definitions of strengths and weaknesses.

The second time round, notice how it feels to

write this list. Notice any resistance you have ("Sure, the book says the lists should be even in length, but the author doesn't know *me*. I really *do* have more flaws than the average person . . ."). Listen to see if you can hear your own negative bias rushing in to interpret everything. Notice if you were quick to dismiss something that any other objective observer would have put on the strengths side.

What is the purpose of taking inventory of your actual strengths and weaknesses?

To change the narrative you have told yourself for years. The voice in your head has been a negative one, telling you what you can't do and why you're not good enough. But it's wrong, and this simple list is evidence of that. Taking inventory allows you to gain an accurate look at yourself, which will help minimize your weaknesses and normalize your strengths. In short, you will feel permission to see yourself in a more positive light than before. You will prove to yourself in a concrete way that your own negative assumptions and narratives can heavily influence your opinion of yourself.

We all have an ability, trait, or habit we can be confident about, one that maybe we're the best in the world at, even. It can be as silly as twisting your tongue or finding parking spaces, but they are all valid talents that give you value and aren't insignificant. We all have something to take pride in and that we would feel comfortable doing in front of a crowd. Every one of us has something to offer, and thinking even beyond gifts and skills we can show off to other people, we are *all* capable of being kind and thoughtful friends, of keeping our word, of working hard, of practicing good habits, or of being supportive of our families. We are all utterly unique individuals who have as much right to take our place in the world as any of the other millions of unique individuals. Have you been consistently downplaying and discounting these things in yourself without realizing it?

By gaining an objective and realistic view of what you are capable of, and of your own innate value as a human being, you can base your confidence level on what is real instead of what is imagined or distorted. Obviously, everyone in the world has weaknesses and things they need improvement on, but confident people allow themselves to identify with their strengths and positive aspects. They understand deep down in their bones that they are just people, and people have both good and bad parts to them. Having flaws doesn't mean you are entirely bad—confident people simply choose to put their goodness at the center of who they are.

If you are honest with yourself, you'll know

exactly what your good traits are. You may also have to battle a compulsion to be modest when listing your strengths. Many of us have grown up being more or less taught to act small, think little of ourselves, and defer to others, especially women. Others have been taught that to embrace and own their own talent and brilliance is selfish and makes others uncomfortable, and so they hide it away for the sake of not drawing attention to themselves. Or, being "modest" could simply be a classic coping mechanism that acts to lower expectations for yourself so you never feel that you fall short. You don't try, you don't fail. In other words, it's an excuse. It's not modesty; it's another place for insecurity to take hold and keep you in your comfort zone.

No matter how you feel today, always remember your strengths, talents, and past achievements. Nothing (real!) has changed to separate you from the person you were that day to the current day where you feel low.

Take inventory to build your confidence, because just like your achievements, these things are evidence of how great you can be and have been in the past. Perhaps of how others see you.

To that end, there's a concept I like to use called the Confidence Resume.

The Confidence Resume isn't a checklist of things you should tell others; it's rather for yourself. And just like a job application resume, you should review and update it periodically. The purpose of the Confidence Resume is to again change the narrative you have of yourself.

When you have this resume created, you'll be able to glance at it and instantly know that you're not actually the type of person you feel you are at the moment. Your low self-confidence is like a distorting filter set on top of your good characteristics, making you look small and bad and weak and insignificant. You're more than that. You're above it, and you have the evidence right in front of you. Every single item on the resume is a fact about yourself, but you've probably suppressed or ignored them while constructing your negative self-narrative.

This is the information that shows you just how great you are, what you've done, the type of person you are, and how impressive you can be. If brainstorming this information was difficult, it's a sign that you probably have an *extremely* negative view of yourself. The more ingrained it is, the longer it will take to unravel, but you can do it—you *will* do it.

It's the difference between telling yourself

you're a good person and being able to list five things that make you a downright impressive person. By having your resume ready for action, you'll be able to battle your inner demons any time you feel low. It's like an emotional inoculation, or a medicine that counteracts the symptoms you experience when you suffer from low self-confidence.

It won't be easy to come up with these on the fly, but that's precisely why it's so important to construct this resume beforehand. You won't be able to think of these immediately, and some of these are buried so deep in your brain, they'll never come up organically. So what exactly goes into the Confidence Resume? This is just a guide; you can come up with your own list, but this works for me and is a great place to start.

- ten most notable accomplishments
- five most unique experiences
- five most impressive moments
- five things you've done that no one else has
- ten things you can do that no one else can

You get the idea. You can keep going, but what we're doing here is taking inventory of your best hits and making them easy to refer to. Looking at the list, which will naturally become impressive and interesting, you can start to realize the type of person you actually are. You're the type of person who climbs huge mountains and was pulled onstage at a Bon Jovi concert! If you met this person out in the world, wouldn't you think they were interesting and want to know them? Well, that person is you. This is the conclusion the evidence leads to. Any other conclusion? It must be in your head.

As you're writing the list, put down everything that makes you feel proud or special or interesting. But you may also notice yourself putting down things that simply make you, you. Your values, your unique perspective on life, your background, the challenges you've overcome, your principles. The fact is, maybe you *don't* come up with any cool anecdotes to share at a party and can't think of much that you've done that others haven't. So what? You are still and will always be the unique person you are. If you're struggling to find enough to put on the list, dig deep. Aren't you working hard to improve yourself? What does this say about your honesty, bravery, and conscientiousness?

Filling your list with things like "I'm kind of hot" and "I have a great haircut" is great, but these things are kind of superficial and can be taken away or lost over time—don't forget to include things that will always be with you. A good sense of humor. Being a just and fair person. Being compassionate and reasonable no matter what. These things are more important than you think. Sometimes, we get carried away with the big-ticket items when compiling our list—we want to tally up the material gains or the impressive ways we can prove to others that we're good enough or even better than them. But true, deep confidence comes from being content and accepting yourself, knowing who you are, and appreciating that.

Take the time to write your list out and go over it regularly. I even encourage people to write it on an index card and carry it around with them as a confidence boost whenever they are contemplating taking action. You've done it before, and you can do it again!

Takeaways:

- Confidence, or lack thereof, plays an integral role in our everyday lives. You likely don't realize the assumptions you make in either position. You may or may not assume people will like or accept you. You may or may not assume that things will go well. You may or may not believe in yourself.
- These are all unfortunate ways in which our mindsets are skewed. Things are made worse because of the part of human psychology that possesses a negativity bias and wants to panic and protect you. This is known as the fight-or-flight response, and it

causes our brains to short circuit by way of the amygdala, and not process things from an objective perspective. It causes our brains to be ruled by fear and terror.

- Social anxiety and low confidence are closely connected, often reinforcing one another. We may feel inferior to others and not equal to the task of putting ourselves out into the world, fearing rejection or discomfort.

- This is further exacerbated by the spotlight effect, which is when we feel that people are always focusing on us and watching our mistakes, causing massive amounts of anxiety and self-consciousness. In fact, this is just a reflection of our own hypervigilance.

- Low confidence can make us believe that others *cause* us to feel the emotions we do. In reality, we perceive an event, and it's our interpretation of it that results in our emotional response. We are responsible for this middle step. If we become conscious of our own negative interpretations, we can take charge of our emotional landscape.

- The brain, the amygdala in particular, is responsible for this negativity bias and our tendency to act automatically and unconsciously. We need to consistently slow down, become aware, and make our thoughts and feelings conscious.

- One confidence-building technique is to

create a Confidence Resume—an objective list of your positive traits and achievements to draw on to counteract negative narratives about yourself.

Chapter 2. Core Beliefs and Automatic Thoughts

Gina has been trying to talk herself into enjoying this work party for about forty-five minutes now. It's not working.

She's sitting in the corner booth of the pub where the party's being held. She's nursing a drink. She's staring at the candle on the table because it's a boring but safe thing to do. She's mastered the art of appearing preoccupied so she doesn't garner attention but also doesn't appear to be wandering aimlessly.

Gina doesn't really want to take the risk of getting into a conversation with someone, anyway, because all they'd see is her funny-looking smile. She thinks her lips contort when she smiles. She believes her smile looks more like a wince. Nobody likes a wincer.

Besides, Gina would fall flat in conversation with any of these people. They're all frightfully smart. A couple of them went to Ivy League colleges. What would an Ivy League graduate have to say to someone like her, who only managed three years in a public state college? Gina thinks she'd only sound stupid.

Brenda, who works in the cubicle adjacent to Gina's, stops by her table. "Why are you hanging out here all by your lonesome self?" Brenda says.

Gina smiles—or, rather, starts to smile—but stops because she hates her smile. "Oh, no reason . . . I just . . . I just started thinking about something, and kind of lost track of time. Sometimes I do that."

Brenda raises an eyebrow. Suddenly Rick from accounting taps Brenda on the shoulder and says, "Darts tournament. Starting now. I hear you're better at aiming pointy things than anyone in marketing." Brenda zips away.

Gina's a bit taken aback. What was that eyebrow raise all about? What in the world did *that* mean? Brenda must think she's way too strange. Maybe it was her awful smile? She must think Gina's selfish sitting all by herself. That's what the eyebrow raise meant: "Who do you think you are?"

Gina can't handle it. She *knew* she didn't belong at this stupid party. She makes her escape from the party without saying goodbye. Later, at home, she beats herself up for being a bit of a loser, and quietly tells herself that other people are not worth it, not worth the risk and the awkwardness. She can't really decide who she hates more—those perfect people at the party or herself.

What started off as a chance to get to know her workmates a little better has turned into what it always has: another weekend night on the sofa, binge-watching *Game of Thrones*, which shows people treating other people far less violently than Gina treats herself.

Where Lack of Confidence Comes From

Gina would be described as suffering from a kind of social anxiety, but at the core of these feelings is a deeper one: the sincere belief that she is fundamentally not worth very much. Because we feel unworthy on a deep level, we feel less than other people, so social interactions may feel like the most difficult of all. We avoid other people because, in some way, we feel worse about ourselves when in context with others who we see as better than us.

A lack of confidence and its close cousin social anxiety are different from most phobias or actions because you can't realistically escape the source of your fears. At some point, you're going to *have* to get out into the world. Most of us have to do so on a daily basis. And yet, even with repeated exposure to social situations, some still can't overcome their lack of confidence and let their anxiety continue. It seems entirely illogical that you wouldn't be able to adjust to something you encounter so frequently. But it's not a logical thing, and there is a very specific thought process that underlies it all that reinforces harmful beliefs.

British psychologists David M. Clark and Adrian Wells devised a "cognitive model" of social anxiety (and the lack of confidence) that treats the affliction as a complex process characterized by fear and insecurity. Clark and Wells described the typical step-by-step mental patterns of someone who is in an active social situation, and when they're ruminating before or after it happens.

In this way, it's frighteningly easy to see how social fears can manifest. And with just a few small tweaks, they can be infinitely worsened or brought back from the brink. They observed how disempowering thoughts began, how they are reinforced, and how they eventually begin to be part of the narrative people tell themselves. To understand this process is to understand how you ended up at this point. The following characteristics are, I'm sure you'll agree, not too different from those of a person with low confidence. They all come from the same basic place: "I'm not enough."

Making assumptions. In the first step, before any actual interaction, a socially anxious person works, so to speak, from a set of expectations and beliefs about themselves and the world they've nurtured, likely since a very young age. These assumptions float to the surface in a social environment, making them extremely difficult to navigate. They are all present in the person before an interaction occurs. Clark and Wells divided these assumptions into three categories:

Assumption 1: High standards. Socially anxious people often impose unreasonable expectations on how they should behave in a communal setting: *"I have to look smart," "I have to be appealing," "I have to sound like an exciting person," "I can't be weak."* These standards go way beyond having good manners—they constitute a harsh checklist of behaviors that cause a great deal of stress. Actually, these border on expectations of perfection and flawlessness. Of course, they are setting themselves up for failure with these expectations. Yup, that's right—nobody actually ever *reaches* these ridiculous heights. Think of these "standards" more as medieval torture devices than legitimate, reachable goals.

Assumption 2: Conditional beliefs. Socially anxious people have deep concern over the outcome of their interactions with others and fear the potential fallout: *"If I don't speak for an extended amount of time, they'll all think I'm boring," "If I say how much I dislike a certain singer, they'll think I have no taste," "If I talk about things in my life, they won't like me."* That's giving a lot of power to other people in the interaction. And anyway, who really decided that this was the case in the first place? You did. Nobody else.

You may attribute cause and effect to situations with no prior justification or evidence. And if you just quietly accept this condition without ever confirming it, you never give yourself the chance to realize that, probably, other people don't agree at all. It's like deciding on some arbitrary rules for how a game is played—and then deliberately making the rules work against you. Silly, huh?

Assumption 3: Unconditional negative beliefs. Low self-opinion—often imprinted from childhood—is major fuel for the socially anxious: *"I'm weird," "I'm dull," "I'm uneducated," "I'm naïve"*—the list goes on. This kind of self-talk can be incredibly tough to overcome since it channels a belief system that's developed and cultivated over years and years. Remember the ripple effect?

But these assumptions are just that—assumptions. It's you making a guess about how the world works. In this case, your guess is wrong. All these assumptions either stem from or are maintained by an underlying belief that you are not good enough, worse than others, or somehow fundamentally bad or wrong.

With these three assumptions at the forefront of the socially anxious person's mind, getting through a social situation can feel like a juggling act. They also need validation that they've executed their self-directives successfully—if they don't get explicit approval from others, they'll take even a neutral response as rejection. When you find someone that operates with these assumptions, you find that there is nowhere for them to go but down into a spiral of negativity.

Intense self-monitoring. In the second step, which occurs during interactions, a socially unconfident person fears negative reactions from those they're associating with. This internal duress transforms them from a person into what Clark and Wells call "a social object." This means that instead of acting in a natural or unforced way, the socially anxious person watches *their own behavior* in the company of others, monitoring themselves as if they were being graded for how well they do. Remember the "spotlight"? And how the spotlight isn't really other people's observation of you, but really a reflection of your own constant self-consciousness and judgement?

Unconfident people are trying to accomplish the impossible task of doing two things at once: interacting and analyzing. They are so busy thinking about doing that they can't really *do*. They are so closely watching their actions, expressions, and words that they scarcely have time to just be, spontaneously.

Predictably, splitting your attention doesn't help get positive reactions from people, and usually just reinforces the fears and assumptions that drive them. It's a vicious cycle. Imagine speaking to a person who seems always distracted, always stilted and unnatural, thinking of what to say next as you speak, or behaving as though interacting with you is incredibly difficult, uncomfortable, and stressful. Doesn't feel good from the other side either, does it?

If a person can see how anxious and uncomfortable you are, they may respond in a certain way, which—you guessed it—gets passed back through the same negative bias filter and interpreted through all your beliefs of yourself as basically terrible . . . repeat until someone ends up on the couch miserably watching *Game of Thrones* again.

Clark and Wells declared three thought patterns that socially anxious and unconfident people use to monitor their conduct. See if you can notice any of these patterns in your own thinking:

Thought pattern 1. "If I feel anxious, I must look anxious." The socially anxious person feels like they must be an open book, and everyone around them can tell when they're going through an episode of great distress. This is just another way that we can assume that our inner experience and the real world are more closely connected than they really are.

Unconfident people believe they exhibit outward displays of tensions like shaking or stammering and the whole room can see them, similar to the spotlight effect. Furthermore, they may think that being found out as a nervous or unconfident person is somehow unforgiveable. But in truth, an outside observer might not even see or notice the person showing such strain. Even if they did, in reality, very few people will judge or be cruel to someone in obvious distress. Would you? Neither would others!

Picture someone who is convinced that everyone else in the room is super relaxed and confident, and only *they* are nervous. This fact in itself ramps up the anxiety, as they constantly equate "they can tell I'm anxious" with "they can tell I don't belong and now hate me." This goes on and on, completely invisibly, until the person is so distressed, they rush out of the room in an awkward way, leaving everyone to wonder what happened. But, up until that moment, everyone in the room was oblivious to anything going on.

Unconfident people will manage to convince themselves of their own downfall, and in doing this, cause it.

Thought pattern 2. Distortion of an observer's perspective. Clark and Wells found that many people suffering from social phobia "appear to experience spontaneously occurring images in which they seem themselves as if viewed from an observer's perspective." But the images returned to the individual aren't ones that objective observers would necessarily have— they come back as gross caricatures of themselves that represent their internal fears. For example, somebody who perceives themselves as overweight might imagine everyone who looks at them sees an elephant. A person who considers themselves emotionally weak might see a vision of themselves as a frail, rickety convalescent.

Thought pattern 3. Fear, distort, and repeat. Clark and Wells defined the third step as a "felt sense." Essentially it means multiplying the fears and distortions of the first two thought patterns until they become a firm part of one's self-belief. This generates and solidifies the negative self-perception of a socially anxious person.

Safety behaviors. Armed with a boatload of mini-phobias and self-monitoring abilities, in the third step, the socially anxious person often develops a catalogue of behaviors that will protect them from breakdown in a social situation. These are "safety behaviors"— exterior behaviors that serve to defend a socially anxious person from what they perceive as potential threats. They're psychological soothers that help them take their mind off their uneasiness or prevent them from taking hold. You might perceive them more clearly by their more widespread name— *defense mechanisms*.

Again, picture someone who is insecure of their stature, who buys a huge truck to attempt to overcompensate and feel "big." They follow these guidelines to the letter, and if they emerge unscathed from a certain social situation, they think it's because they were careful and guarded—*not* because they were never in any danger to begin with, as is often the case.

Many times, a person will deploy safety behaviors in a sort of "package," since their anxieties often come from a diverse number of multiple sources and forms. The multiple actions form a kind of playbook, a series of checked behaviors to be dispatched at various points in the social setting.

For example, take someone who is utterly terrified of looking stupid. They fear their alleged stupidity will manifest itself in various ways:

"I'll sound stupid when I talk." To combat this fear, their safety behavior might be to aggressively search for interesting topics at home to bring up in conversation, or continually turn the topic back to them and their accomplishments. Charming.

"They'll make fun of me." The person might try to look imposing or tough in a forced way.

"They'll know I don't understand what they're talking about." To cover this up, they'll pretend to nod along with everything that is said, and never admit that they don't know something.

Clark and Wells noted that some of these safety behaviors are, in fact, self-defeating—by over-executing them, a person could cause the very symptom or blunder they're trying to avoid. Indeed, even though the behaviors are intended to protect, they are almost always dead giveaways for overcompensation and a lack of confidence.

The intense amount of self-monitoring that accompanies safety behaviors can also start a self-aware loop of attention that could draw the person more inward and out of a normal social situation. And being hyper-aware of their anxieties and appearance can also make *others* notice that something's off. In this sense, the social phobic makes a self-fulfilling prophecy: they're so aware of their shortcomings and criticism that they cause them.

Misreading social cues. In the fourth step, from an accumulation of all the previous steps, the socially anxious person tends to view their current situation and everyone around them in a negative light. That means they're likely to misread the reactions of other people as rejections or criticisms—even if they're neutral. For example, if someone they're telling a story to laughs because they said something funny, they might instead interpret the laughter as mocking or rude.

Many suffering from social anxiety have set-in-stone ideas about how people should act in social situations, and quickly notice when someone falls short of those usually unspoken standards. They judge even the most neutral or vague reactions as negative responses. The person telling the funny story, for example, might think their listener should be focused on them with full eye contact. If whoever they're speaking to looks away for a second or exhibits a facial reaction, they consider it a message of disapproval. Sadly, they are viewing everything through a negative filter, so even the best of intentions can and will be interpreted to be malicious and a reason for low confidence. These are cognitive distortions, which we will cover in greater depth in the next chapter.

Analyzing before and after social situations. In the final step, and the completion of the cycle, the social phobic/confidence-challenged tend to agonize and ruminate about social situations—even when they're not actively in them at the moment.

The lead-up to a social event can stir up great anxiety for a social phobic. They might spend a considerable amount of time worrying about what might transpire down to the last insignificant detail. They'll remember previous encounters that were disappointing or negative to them. They'll imagine they'll fail spectacularly in the upcoming event. They'll forecast being dismissed or spurned by others in the group. This is before they've even put their shoes on to leave.

After the event is over, the social phobic will feel at least some relief from their anxiety since they're out of the stressful situation. Indeed, it will feel something like escaping from a lion's den. But it won't be long until the post-mortem starts. The social phobic goes back over every interaction they had at the event, recalling their heightened anxiety and the small telling details that get set in their memory, and filtering every exchange and occurrence through their negative self-opinions. They'll classify the event among all the other occasions in which they felt they failed. Essentially, they are looking for (or sometimes completely fabricating) evidence for the core belief that they already "know" is true, i.e. *I'm not worth very much.*

People with higher self-confidence? They don't engage in these distortions or interpretations or ruminations. They are more likely to simply engage with situations as they really are, without laying a negative narrative over it like a bad filter. What they are able to do is regulate their own emotions. They don't have automatic negative interpretations, and if they do (for example, "He thinks I'm an idiot"), they immediately counter it with something more neutral and rational ("No, that can't be true. I have no evidence for that!").

They have, in other words, a strong and well-functioning "emotional immune system." They simply never allow harmful thoughts or interpretations to gain too strong a hold on them, and reject negative narratives almost like the body rejects pathogens or toxins to stay healthy. Luckily for us, we can strengthen and develop our own emotional immune systems.

Challenging Your Core Beliefs

Core beliefs are part of our psychological networks. They're instilled at an early age and reinforced by our experiences. That's why they're hard to nail down—they are how you view the world; no conscious effort comes from them. They're built in just like the rings of a tree are built in as the tree grows. Things that happen in the past are long gone, and yet, we still feel their effects on us through triggering events and emotional distress. They live on in the stories we tell ourselves . . . which eventually crystallize into our fixed sense of who we are.

Challenging and changing them from an analytical perspective is what is known as cognitive behavioral therapy, or CBT for short. The main strategy of CBT is to teach people how to deal with their negative core beliefs head on, and reprogram them into something less harmful.

There are two primary methods for intervention in the cycle of low confidence. The first is *cognitive restructuring*—a technique for identifying negative cognitive patterns and untrue assumptions we make about ourselves and altering them. Common untrue assumptions have to do with our own lack of competence in a given scenario, or with other people's judgments of us.

Cognitive restructuring is a treatment intended to show people why they are getting stuck in these negative feedback loops and what they can do to significantly alter their thought and behavior patterns in order to remove themselves from the vicious cycle. By recognizing a negative thought pattern and understanding why it persists, we can react differently to it and steer ourselves in a positive direction.

How does one build their awareness about their counterproductive thoughts, emotions, and behaviors? Generally, the first step of those methods entails identifying subconscious thoughts—the ones providing us with a continuous commentary on our experiences as we are living them. These thoughts are constantly affecting our moods because we tend to simply accept them as accurate reflections of reality and ourselves.

When we stop accepting the narrative being written by our subconscious, we are able to begin considering alternative points of view. Suddenly the cycle is broken, or at least altered. This leads to a more sensible and stable way of thinking about whatever it is causing us distress at any given time, preventing us from falling into those vicious cycles mentioned earlier.

By simply considering alternative possibilities, we can balance out our emotions and thoughts and reduce the sadness and hopelessness that occurs when we get trapped in a negative feedback loop. This, in turn, enables us to engage in behaviors and activities that promote our well-being, pulling us out of our dark mindset and making us stronger and better.

Few people are actively aware of their thinking patterns, even though they engage in these patterns every day. CBT allows you to address errors in your thinking to correct your behavior and in turn change your life. You might assume that you require a therapist, or at least an incredibly patient friend to conduct CBT, but that's where thought diaries and worksheets come into play.

The concept of the thought diary was borne from the desire to identify the core beliefs that inform our actions and emotions. It uncovers the relationships between our behavior, thoughts, and feelings. Basically, it's the process of cognitive behavioral therapy, and actually similar to how a counselor might help one get to the root of their psychological issues.

A typical entry in a thought diary outlines a triggering event or thought, the self-messaging that comes from it, and the resultant emotions that emerge. Sifting through all this information brings up your core beliefs so you can challenge them. Remember, we want to try to isolate and analyze the automatic thoughts we have and replace them with healthier versions.

Steps in a thought diary entry can be arranged in the easy-to-remember A-B-C format— although for the purposes of this process, it's actually A-C-B:

Activating Event. This is simply the origin point of your emotional change. It could be an actual, physical event. But it could also be an internal event—a thought, memory, or mental image. It's whatever caused your emotional status to change from calm to agitation:

- Hearing an old song that reminds you of someone you were close to

- Running into an old friend on the street

- Being criticized by a supervisor

- Remembering being bullied by a high school classmate

Consequences. In this step, you identify the specific emotions and sensations that arose. These could be simple feeling words— "anxious," "unhappy," "sickened," "panicky," "melancholy," "confused," and so forth. To get more specific about the emotions involved, you may want to rate how intensely you felt them on whatever scale works for you. Maybe you were sixty-five percent panicky and thirty-five percent confused. Your feelings of sickness may have been a ten and your anxiety may have been a five. Underline or circle which emotion was most relevant.

Beliefs. This is where the action begins. How do you link the activating event with the consequences? What unconscious narrative or story about yourself was told to achieve the consequence? What leaps in logic or to conclusions were being made to get you to your current negative state? Getting to the bottom of these beliefs involves some drilling of yourself with progressive questioning until you finally get to the bottom of your situation—your core beliefs:

- "What was I thinking?"

- "What was going through my head when this happened?"

- "What's wrong with that?"

- "What does this all mean?"

- "What does it reveal about me?"

Yes, it's a lot of work, and you might struggle at points to obtain the answers you're looking for.

But the effort to peel away layers of self-messaging will eventually pay off. When your investigation finally brings you face to face with your core beliefs, that's when you can start the process of challenging them.

Let's take a couple examples of seemingly benign activating events and put them through the ABC ringer. They may seem a bit abbreviated, but you'll find that they closely mirror real-life situations.

1. Steve is having a conversation with his new friend Emily at a table at a bar. They're having a good talk until Steve's acquaintance Jack walks up, pulls up a chair, and starts chatting, oblivious to the fact that he stopped Steve and Emily's conversation cold. Steve is angry. You won't like him when he is angry.

Steve's activating event is Jack stopping his conversation. That's easy.

What is the consequence—what did this event activate, feelings-wise? He felt flustered, for one. That was probably the dominant emotion. He'd give it an "eight" on a scale of one to ten. He also sensed feelings of anger and frustration, but not quite as powerfully as the panic. Maybe a "four." He felt the front of his head get a little heavy. Steve qualifies that as "confusion." But he's not sure why, so he gives them a "three."

Now Steve has to figure out why this particular event made him freak out. Does he dislike Jack? No, not at all, he decides. He's an okay guy, if sometimes a little over-excitable.

So, Steve asks himself what was going through is head at the time. He was having a good conversation with Emily, feeling like they were both talking earnestly and actively about things they're both interested in. And then it got interrupted. He felt flustered.

Why? Because he was disappointed that the conversation was derailed, and that Jack wasn't self-aware enough to know he was interrupting.

What does that mean? He feels that Jack was being careless about his ego and personality and thought nothing of imposing his will over Jack's.

Why is that? Because Steve doesn't think he asserts himself enough.

And why is that? Because Steve believes he's too modest to ever be able to do that.

And what does that mean? Steve doesn't feel he deserves respect, and Jack's interruption was just a reminder that he doesn't deserve it.

That's Steve's core belief: he has little if any self-regard and thinks he lets people take advantage of his recessive nature to "bowl him over" and take over his social situations without regard to what he really wants. Because of that, he doesn't see himself as somebody respectable. In other words, his problem is a low self-esteem or lack of confidence. It's not easy to reach this point just from analyzing a reaction to an interruption, but that's how you come to the point of understanding and changing your core beliefs.

2. Joann is meeting up with Amanda, a good friend she hasn't seen in over a year, at a coffee shop. When Amanda shows up, Joann happily waves her to her table. Amanda gives a weak smile, walks over, and gives her a light embrace. Joann is surprised that Amanda wasn't as enthusiastic to see her after such a long time. In fact, Joann feels downright rejected over it and decides to reject Amanda in kind by leaving after ten minutes.

Joann's activating event was Amanda's apparent indifference when they embraced.

What is the consequence—how did that make Joann feel? A little confused, maybe a little disheartened. She felt her stomach drop a little, which she usually interprets as disappointment.

What was going through Joann's head? She felt like she was being rejected. She felt like she had over-invested in an emotional expectation that wasn't returned in kind. She felt that such a good friend would be overjoyed to see someone after such a long time. She created her own expectations and unfairly placed them on other people. She started to tell herself a story about how nobody ever really wanted to be her friend, because why would they? Her lack of confidence is immediately in the picture, steering a negative interpretation.

How had she over-invested? She thought that Amanda's enthusiasm would match her own. If she had known different, she wouldn't have appeared to be so happy. This made her feel silly, like a puppy who was happy to see her master.

Why? Because Joann thinks she might have driven some people away with her over-enthusiastic expressions of emotion.

Why? Because she senses some people tend to pull away when she appears to be excited.

Why? Because she's too weird to have close friends.

That is Joann's core belief: She's strange, and it alienates people. Not only that, despite her best efforts, she is still too weird for even people like Amanda to care about. And here, "strange" is just another word for "bad." Again, we come to this point from an innocuous reaction on the part of Amanda, who for her part may have just avoided a car accident or received an urgent email from work. The possibilities are endless, and yet Joann wanted to find the interpretation that was harmful and fit her narrative about herself.

Once you practice this technique yourself, you may be surprised to discover just how often things are not what they seem at first. Anger is often fear in disguise. Overly critical attitudes toward others can conceal a lack of personal self-esteem, and avoidance or apathy is often the mask that low confidence wears. It's no exaggeration to say that most challenges in life are caused in some way by a deeply rooted belief in our own lack of worth, which then manifests in countless ways. Address that unconfident root and all its symptoms disappear.

Finding Alternate Beliefs

Now you've gotten to the bottom of your situation and figured out what your core beliefs are. At this point, you might think the effort to change them into more workable, alternate beliefs might be futile—after all, these beliefs have likely informed a great deal of your behavioral and thought patterns. Maybe it's too late to change them.

This is the exact moment to start challenging these very beliefs. It's a process in which you draw upon your entire range of experiences to determine when the core belief in question was, in fact, untrue.

The first step is writing down one of the core beliefs you've just uncovered. Ask yourself what experiences you've had that prove your core belief wasn't always true. Generate as many experiences as you can and be very specific about what happened. Don't worry if you're not entirely sure these experiences were totally applicable—just list them all.

Using these past experiences as a guide, you can now produce a more balanced, healthier core belief that will hopefully replace the one that's been the source of your distress.

Let's take Steve's core belief from above, that he doesn't deserve respect. He writes that down on a piece of paper.

He tries to remember times when he *did* earn respect. He remembers when he was in college and viewed as a great philosophy student. Classmates seemed to like his answers and asked him for help in understanding their coursework. On a social level, Steve remembers a few times when he was appreciated for giving sound advice to friends who needed help, how many times they laughed at his jokes, and how clever they thought he was.

There you go, Stevie boy! You *do* have a track record of respect. People like you and want to hear you out. Sometimes other people aren't aware of boundaries, but that's their issue and not a reflection of how much respect you deserve. When you can find a whole boatload of evidence to the contrary of your negative core belief—an inevitability—then it almost can't be argued with. Emotionally, you may still identify with the negative core belief, but little by little, you can accept a different story about yourself—the truth.

Steve's new core belief might go something like this: "I deserve and have earned respect in the past. I just need to remember that sometimes other people aren't entirely aware of my situation, and it's not a reflection on me or my deserving to be respected."

Now let's consider Joann's core belief: that she's too strange. Well, first of all, she remembers her parents when she was growing up, and how they taught her never to feel she needed to conform to others. She also remembers a few times when people admired her creative solutions and unfettered expression of herself.

She remembers a friend from high school telling her how she inspired her to "color outside the lines," and that it made a real difference in her life. In addition, she happens to know that Amanda hasn't had an easy year—she suffered a breakup and has grown increasingly frustrated at work. Is she actually strange, and does that harm her relationships?

Joann's new core belief? "I'm unusual and like to do things in my own way. I'm not strange—and if I am, it's in a good way. Sometimes other people aren't in a position to appreciate my uncommon viewpoint, but that's all right."

Nietzsche famously said, "The great epochs of our life come when we gain the courage to rechristen our evil as what is best in us." So, to challenge your negative core beliefs, you don't necessarily have to contradict them. The opposite of the belief "I'm a worthless worm" is not "I'm a perfect demigod" but "I am a complex individual with both good and bad sides, and I'm worthy of love and acceptance as I am."

You are the one telling the story. What kind of story would you like to tell about yourself? When we are unconfident, we are telling a story in which we're the bad guy. But you can change that story. Can you "rechristen" the story of you being a weak, contemptible loser into one where you are sensitive, kind, and unique? Instead of seeing your knee-jerk tendency to criticize yourself as an unchanging law of the universe, can you rechristen it as a small, lovable flaw in your personality, and something that you're working on and getting better at every day?

More Experimentation on Your Core Beliefs

Another way to determine the validity—or falsehood—of your core belief is to conduct a sort of trial or experiment. This also challenges your core belief using a deliberate step-by-step process:

- Write down the core belief you're examining.

- Think of ways that you can put that belief to the test. These are actual tasks that you can perform.

- Then, write down what you expect or predict will happen after conducting these tasks *if* your core belief was true.

- Perform the tasks.

- Write down what really happened after you completed your task.

- Compare and contrast your predictions with what actually happened.

- Finally, document what you learned from the task and come up with a new, more reasonable core belief that goes in line with your discoveries.

For example, let's take Joann's self-belief that she's too strange for mass consumption. She writes it down. "I'm too strange."

How can Joann put this to the test?

- She decides to ask her parents what they thought about her "strangeness" as an adult.

- She could ask some of her friends who she really trusts as well.

- She also has a creative idea: to write a blog about her "history as a nonconformist," and see what others' reactions are.

What does she think will happen?

- Her parents are going to support her no matter what.

- Most of her friends are going to say they like her originality, and always have. She has a really strait-laced friend named Andrea who sometimes seems "curious" about her quirkiness, so she expects she'll respond noncommittally.

- The blog, frankly, she doesn't expect a lot of response from because she's not sure how many people really visit it. But it's worth a shot.

What actually happens?

- Her parents supported her.

- *All* of her friends said they loved her because of her originality, not in spite of it. And Andrea was arguably the most enthusiastic; she just doesn't emote that much.

- Joann's blog receives a healthy number of positive responses—and a couple of thank-yous for saying things that others really wanted to hear.

After writing those results down, Joann compares and contrasts her expectations with her results. What did she learn? She has the grounding support she's always had, maybe a little more. That her main issue may simply be not trusting her originality *enough*, and that she should put it out there more often. And even though she considers herself "strange," in actuality, she's got a valuable alternative viewpoint that people need to hear more of.

Finally, Joann documents her findings. Probably in a blog, since that's kind of her thing. No one is going to promise that this is an easy process, or that you can perform this once and immediately be cured of your negative beliefs. After all, they are so powerfully ingrained that you don't even realize when you use them, so it's going to take time and repetition to conquer them. What's important is that the process has begun—a recognition of what you are dealing with, a recognition that it does not represent reality, and a recognition of a more accurate and positive self-perception.

Shut Up!

Doing all this work on your core belief system may sound exhausting, and it certainly can be. You might get to a point where you just can't contend with all the issues that are coming up, or can't handle them as they're constantly coming up. Maybe you just need to take a rest from working on your social anxieties. Or maybe you just need to stop talking about them constantly.

This might be a great time to shut up already.

Researchers once discovered that nursing negative emotions can be habit-forming. As unlikely as it sounds, sorrow, failure, regret, and dissatisfaction can actually be sources of calm and reassurance. Another study even suggested that grievous experiences even activate the brain's pleasure centers.

One reason this might be true is we're afraid of not being able to feel. We'd rather be feeling *something*—even if it's sadness, pain, or disappointment—than *nothing.* "I'm gonna hurl myself against the wall," musician Warren Zevon once sang, "'cause I'd rather feel bad than feel nothing at all." At least painful emotions remind us that we can still feel, that we are in fact alive. We fear slipping into a state where nothing affects us at all.

For this reason, a lot of people thrive on creating drama. They verbalize their problems in the hopes of catharsis and relief. They tell anybody who's around every detail about their issues and complaints. They go on and on. Talking about their problems makes them feel important. This can help, and misery certainly loves company.

But at the same time, over-sharing one's litanies of pain and frustration can exaggerate the importance of the problem. Constantly sharing your negative experiences also creates a kind of regenerating monster of despair—the more you talk about them, the more you replay the problems in your brain, and the more you feed the beast that produces all your torment, pessimism and despair. It's the proverbial hydra from Greek mythology—if you cut off its head, two more will grow in its place. If you're the type who overstates or amplifies your issues— "making a mountain out of a molehill," as it's called—this is especially the case.

To reset your emotions, maybe you should consider dialing it down a little and just not talking about your problems for a bit. Forget catharsis and even think about suppression and forgetting for a second. It sounds counterproductive and the opposite of what we're always told to do, but there's some science to back this proposal.

Dr. Brad Bushman, a professor of communication, conducted a study in which he instructed his subjects to write an essay about a troublesome or touchy subject. Their papers were turned in to the test administrators, who then "graded" the essays in remarkably cruel ways. The researchers gave extraordinarily tough feedback—some were told their papers were "one of the worst they had ever read."

After they'd been raked over the coals, some of the participants were given the option to take out their frustrations on a punching bag for two minutes. The rest of the subjects weren't given that opportunity and did nothing. Next, all the participants took part in a "game" in which they had the option to attack a fictional "opponent" with blasts of noise. Researchers used the noises produced to gauge the participants' levels of hostility.

Bushman's researchers believed that the subjects who took out their feelings on the punching bag would successfully "release" their anger, and that the subjects who did nothing would be more aggressive in the noise-blasting game. But the exact opposite happened: the bag-punchers carried their anger over into the noise-blasting game, attacked their opponents with longer, louder barrages of ear-curdling sound. Catharsis wasn't necessarily what was reached through expression of emotion.

Bushman's results imply that sometimes the best course of action after being provoked to anger is to just sit quietly and let it pass. An angry person taking out their frustration in a physical manner doesn't really help them experience a catharsis or calm down. Rather, establishing a connection between anger and physical aggression *multiplies* the anger. The negativity and the act of hostility only link together more strongly.

Left unchecked, this kind of anger can begin to feel natural—even pleasant. The anger has become a source of power because it's been associated with physical aggression. This in turn inflates and strokes the ego. Then little miniature acts of brutality or sadism start to become appealing—trash-talking, provoking others, revenge. You start to revel in other people's misery or failure, a feeling the German language calls *schadenfreude*. You feel joy when someone you don't like goes through something bad— "karma," you call it.

All this is masking your own insecurities, but they're all very much still there. You've settled on a program of total command because you're actually terrified. It feels better when you can convince other people to be terrified of *you*.

Let's consider this same dynamic when it comes to lack of confidence. If a situation or person triggers you into a spiral of self-criticism and anxious rumination, you can actually just mentally say to yourself "stop" and distract yourself. Once negative self-talk and self-hating sentiments are in full swing, you can, in a strange way, feel vindicated. You may feel like you're just being honest and real, expressing your truth. But what you're doing is wallowing and giving yourself a VIP pass to a mega pity party.

It's like the reverse of a pep talk. Some people sit down and list out everything that's wrong with them in prolonged detail, or tell the same story over and over again as if to confirm, "Yes, I am the victim, and yes, this is a very, very terrible situation." Now, there's not even a point in dissecting *why* "misery loves company" or why we masochistically engage in this sort of rumination—at the end of the day, the best thing is just to cut it out. Don't feed the cycle.

Over-concentration on negativity ultimately fails, even if it feels like a weird kind of satisfaction in the short term. The idea that beating yourself up will somehow "purge" the bad feelings and stop them from rising up is utterly false. In truth, the opposite happens: your negativity just gets stronger, almost like it gets absorbed into your bloodstream. Being angry or self-pitying or unconfident becomes addictive. When you reach that point, it's vital to stop the circuit of negativity and start channeling positivity as soon as you can.

This is where shutting up comes in handy. I'm *not* talking about repressing your emotions or acting against your feelings. That's also unhealthy. Efforts to be positive are always great, but recognition of our negative emotions also keeps us grounded and vigorous. You really can't have one without the other.

But "purging" negative emotions doesn't vacate them—it only gives that negativity new life. You're giving your negativity its own show. This holds you back from real emotional growth. And it can even result in tangible damage to your brain: a Stanford research project determined that a half hour of either hearing or issuing complaints can cause harm to the hippocampus, a small brain organ that helps to regulate memories.

There's a direct link between social anxiety and negativity. A 2016 Australian research study showed that "elevated social anxiety vulnerability is characterized only by facilitated attentional engagement with socially negative information." Obsessing over negative details—including by constantly talking about one's problems—only reinforces one's social fears and does nothing to inspire real confidence in a social setting.

Obviously, I'm not saying you should never discuss your problems with anybody else. But do so in a reserved fashion and back off the melodrama. We all know it's unhealthy to bottle things inside, lest you explode like a volcano at a later time. But that's not what is being suggested. It's simply to not air all your grievances all the time, because instead of finding catharsis, you'll have created a cesspool of negativity and unhappiness to live in.

Later in the book, we're going to consider a brilliant anecdote for overcoming this kind of impotent negativity—doing something about it. Taking action is a powerful antidote to wallowing or rehashing the same tired stories. It's good to share feelings, to communicate your reality, and to know that it's okay to feel bad sometimes. But occasionally, you might want to ask, "What am I actually *doing* about this problem?" If the answer is "absolutely zilch," then you know it's time to either give it a rest or transform your negativity into meaningful action.

Save your problem-sharing for people you know you trust—and who won't let you turn your negativity into a freak show. Speak to them as a friend, not an audience member. If that's not possible—and I say this with all attendant helpfulness—you might want to think about putting a cork in it.

Takeaways:

- Core beliefs are at the root of your lack of confidence. They can manifest in many ways. Typically, they come from a set of automatic thoughts that have been occurring since childhood that you have never analyzed or corrected. Thus, you don't know anything different, or less detrimental, to yourself. This is characterized by faulty assumptions, self-monitoring, and safety behaviors, all of which compound on each other.

- The way to change your patterns of thought is to challenge your core beliefs and automatic thoughts, and this is done through a process called cognitive behavioral therapy, or CBT. CBT is the act of observing your thoughts, and the method we will be talking about is aptly called *cognitive restructuring*. We are all driven by unconscious beliefs and assumptions that influence our actions, and this is a process aimed at making this work for our benefit.

- For our purposes, CBT takes the form of using a thought diary to examine an ACB process: activating event, consequence, and belief. The important part is to understand the belief, because that is what unlocks confidence, or the lack thereof. Then, replace that belief with a more factual, accurate, and empowering one.

- Finally, even though it's healthy and sometimes necessary to speak of what ails us, there is a limit. Anxiety tends to build on anxiety, so when you continue to speak out and ruminate about your worries, you are not seeking catharsis anymore, you are placing yourself into a spiral of negativity and unhappiness. Simply STOP—tell these thoughts to shut up and move on!

Chapter 3. Cognitive Distortions

Our perception of the world is ninety-nine percent incorrect. There's no other way around it. What we see is often not the reality that exists, and that's completely normal. Of course, this is a continuation of the prior chapter's discussion of flawed beliefs and patterns of thought.

Our perceptions of the world around us are inaccurate because of one thing in particular: they are based on biases and perspectives we bring from our past. In other words, they are not based on how things *are*, but how we think things are, according to how they *used to be*. To go even further, they may be based on memories of past events that, truthfully, we didn't quite perceive accurately in the first place.

Unfortunately, in general, these misperceptions shed light on our insecurities and rob us of our confidence and power. If we had early childhood experiences that taught us to think of ourselves as inferior, unlikable, or worthless, then our personalities and worldview grow around these assumptions. When we encounter new situations or people, we pass these experiences through our (distorted) worldview and interpret it according to what we already "know."

If we *know* we are worthless, then not getting a promotion means we don't deserve one and will never get one. It also means that if we *do* get one, we think it must be a mistake, or that people must feel sorry for us. Cognitive distortions are like those warped funhouse mirrors—they are reflecting reality, but not as it truly is.

For instance, we may unfairly compare ourselves to others or focus on the most negative aspects of a situation—a suspicion that a spouse or partner is cheating due to a grueling work schedule, or the assumption that you are not liked because a friend lost their phone and didn't reply within an hour. There are alternative explanations, but the flawed perception is there nonetheless, preventing us from seeing that alternative.

To become more confident, you must change the way that you view the world. Another way of saying this is to take your own word for it! Information and events come to us in a neutral state; it is only through our interpretation that these items have positive or negative connotations. How we choose to view events determines our realities and has the ability to completely undermine your confidence and will to persevere. Sometimes, we spend a lot of energy trying to change what we think is ugly and misshapen, when what we really should be changing is the wonky mirror we're using to look at ourselves.

A *cognitive distortion* is a view of reality that is negative, pessimistic, and generally incorrect. It can damage your self-esteem, lower your confidence, and make you feel as if you have no control over your life. Cognitive distortion is also a form of self-talk that is damaging and can become so ingrained and habit-forming that people don't realize they are creating an alternate reality where they are destined for unhappiness and a lack of confidence.

Most of us have enough trouble with reality; distorting our view of the world to be more menacing and difficult just saps our confidence and will unnecessarily.

Here's an example. While returning from the restroom, Craig walked past a closed-door meeting in his supervisor Max's office. As he passed by the glass door, he noticed that almost all of his coworkers were in the room, and many glanced in his direction.

He immediately began to feel nervous. Were they talking about him? Had he done something wrong? He was probably going to be fired! Last week, he noticed Sheila and Katie giggling and looking at him in the break room. And the Nickerby account had just moved to another company. He was probably going to get fired, and it would be impossible to find another job because he would definitely be getting a horrible recommendation. He wouldn't be able to make his truck payment next month without a job; it would probably get repossessed.

Craig was in a downward spiral for the rest of the day, worrying about his future work prospects and how he would survive without his usual income while looking for a new job.

The next morning was Craig's birthday, and he was feeling very depressed. He dragged himself into work, prepared for the worst. As soon as he sat down at his desk, he heard a loud, "Surprise! Happy birthday, Craig!" All of his coworkers were gathered behind his desk, armed with small gifts. Sheila rushed over and blurted out, "We've been planning this surprise for weeks! We thought we had been caught when you walked past Max's office yesterday, but it looks like we really surprised you."

Craig was suffering from severe cognitive distortion. Can you guess how?

His perception of an event, a meeting of many of his coworkers, was colored by his negative viewpoint. Although his coworkers were ultimately planning a surprise birthday party, Craig jumped to conclusions and assumed the worst. This cognitive distortion served to lower Craig's self-esteem and put him into a panic mode in which he wasted his energy and time worried about an unlikely future scenario.

In this case, Craig got to see undeniable evidence that his worries were all for nothing. But think about this, how many times have you worried endlessly about something, when in reality, it could have been as harmless as the situation in this example? How much time, energy, and peace of mind have we all wasted by deliberately choosing to put ourselves through this kind of unnecessary torment?

What Are Cognitive Distortions?

In 1976, psychologist Aaron Beck was the first to propose the theory behind cognitive distortions. It wasn't until the 1980s that David Burns popularized it with common names and examples of the distortions. Cognitive distortions are the ways in which your mind convinces you of something that isn't true.

They are usually used to reinforce pessimistic thinking or negative emotions, and we often tell ourselves things that sound rational and accurate yet only serve to emphasize our self-doubt or lack of confidence. So, if we have an inbuilt belief in ourselves as inferior, we adopt a set of cognitive tricks that make it so that everywhere we look, we see evidence and proof for our inferiority. Sound similar to our core beliefs from the previous chapter?

The first step to launching a counterattack on these negative thoughts is by noticing when you are having them. Then you must make a conscious effort to turn them off or find alternative explanations for your worries. By refuting or turning off this negative thinking over and over again, the negative thoughts will diminish over time and automatically be replaced by more rational, balanced thinking. It is only through constant vigilance that you can replace the bad habit of cognitive distortion with the good habit of positive thinking. Be warned that the most stubborn and damaging distortions and core beliefs are often those that seem most invisible or obvious!

Many of us may notice this type of internal dialogue while at work. A nagging thought telling you you're inferior to your colleagues based on their level of education in comparison to yours, a worry about your public speaking skills before a big meeting, or a concern that your boss prefers to give big projects to your coworkers are all examples of cognitive distortions.

All three worries are negative thoughts that likely have no basis in reality. Choosing to stop these thoughts and give them a more positive spin will eventually cause them to be replaced by more logical and balanced thinking. But you have to be consciously aware of those negative thought patterns in the first place in order to do anything meaningful about them.

Confident individuals know that to perceive reality clearly and without unnecessary emotional turmoil, they have to turn off the pessimistic or negative cognitive distortions.

So, for Craig, the experience above could teach him to second-guess his knee-jerk negative reactions to neutral events. This allows for clear, logical thought and advancement socially in the workplace and in relationships. Let's say he makes it a policy to never assume. He notices himself falling into a negativity spiral and deliberately stops it, forcing himself to answer the question: "Do I have any *hard evidence* that any of these assumptions are true?" Seeing that he actually doesn't, he distracts himself away from those thoughts, knowing that they are nothing more than distortions.

Next, we cover a few of the most common cognitive distortions, illustrate them with examples, and discuss how they are detrimental to your sense of confidence. You'll probably recognize more than a few in your own thinking.

Types of Cognitive Distortions

All-or-Nothing Thinking

"Gosh, I haven't read a single book this month, and my goal was to read three! I'm horrible at sticking to goals. If I can't read three books, I may as well not read at all."

"I chewed with my mouth open that one time. How could I have done that? How disgusting. No one will ever be with someone like me. Tasha is going to break up with me tomorrow, I just know it."

All-or-nothing thinking can also be called tunnel vision. This type of cognitive distortion occurs when you focus only on the good or the bad and use that to judge an entire situation, instead of taking a balanced viewpoint. There is only black and white, which can cause you to severely overreact either way.

As fictional race car driver Ricky Bobby in *Talladega Nights* said, "If you ain't first, you're last." Obviously, there are many positions between first and last. Although earning second or third place isn't ideal, there is a huge difference between running a 2:19 marathon and a 4:52. It's vital to not lose sight of the middle ground because all-or-nothing thinking destroys confidence. Not reaching your goal doesn't immediately signal the end of your world as you know it, and consequences that seem enormous and irreversible rarely are.

This attitude is, in a way, quite fragile. By focusing only on the extremes of good and bad, you lose sight of the bigger picture and make yourself extra vulnerable to disappointment, failure, or delay. For confidence, zoom out and look at the goals and events in your life on a larger scale. Understand that there are grey areas, that some things come with a learning curve, and that one small mistake doesn't mean that everything everywhere is ruined forever. By getting caught up in all-or-nothing thinking, this sort of large-scale view is lost and small issues can suddenly feel greatly magnified.

All-or-nothing thinking also manifests itself through lists of ironclad rules about behavior or expectations. People who break these rules make us feel angry, and in turn, if we break a rule, we feel guilty. Lists of "should" or "musts" such as "I must go to the gym every day" or "I must arrive at work at least fifteen minutes before my shift begins" might sound motivational, but they leave little room for compromise or adjustment if life events get in the way of your plan. And actually, you're more likely to perform better if you factor in a little wiggle room here and there, rather than "throwing the baby out with the bath water."

All of these tendencies create a set of expectations that you are destined to fall short of. And when this happens on a continual basis, you can't help but feel inadequate and mediocre at best. But you forget that all these expectations and demands were put there by *you*, not by the world. It was you who agreed to play by the unconscious rule that "unless you are perfect, you are worthless."

To overcome the cognitive distortion of all-or-nothing thinking, you must challenge yourself to see the middle ground. You need to practice compromise and learn to tolerate uncertainty, incompleteness, and imperfection—in ourselves and others. This is, after all, the only place where life actually plays out. You should take into account other viewpoints and strive to see different interpretations of the situation. What does your best friend or father think?

What other solutions or ways to approach the problem can you envision? Can you list three positives to balance out the negatives you've fixated on thus far?

Perfectionism and rigid black-and-white thinking are at their core the opposite of resilience and can be thought of as a coping mechanism for the messiness and unpredictability of life. But, we are allowed to be imperfect (spoiler: you already are), and we can also respond to this inevitable fact with grace, humor, and acceptance (spoiler: there's ultimately not much of a choice!).

Push yourself to think outside of the box to come up with as many interpretations as possible. Even if they seem wacky, having more options forces you to think outside of the cognitive distortion. Confidence means knowing that you can *afford to* mess up. You can make a stupid mistake and still be awesome. Just because you don't know what you're doing today doesn't mean it's impossible to hit it out of the park tomorrow. When everything seems bleak and negative, this realization will cause you to be a bit kinder to yourself.

"Ultimately, it is better to read one or two books than it is to read nothing. Maybe I'll just start with one chapter tonight and see what happens."

"I have so many admirable qualities; that's why Tasha fell in love with me. Chewing with my mouth open is really a pretty minor problem, and I rarely do it."

Personalizing

"Why can't our daughter Marsha hold down a job? She is constantly moving from company to company. I think she was even fired from this last position. I must have done something wrong as a parent. If only we had sent her to Laurelswood High School instead of the public school, this never would have happened! It's all my fault. I should have quit my job and just been there for her."

"I feel terrible that Patricia overcooked the pot roast. If only Jeremy and I hadn't been thirty minutes late for the dinner party. If only I had told him to hurry, this wouldn't have happened! I take full responsibility for this. I should have cooked everything myself."

Personalization is the mother of guilt. In the cognitive distortion of personalizing, you feel responsible for events that cannot conceivably be your fault. While it is admirable to take responsibility for your actions, there are things completely out of your control: the subway schedule, other people's actions, and a million day-to-day factors.

If you have low confidence and are walking around with a jumbo-sized core belief that you are deep down a Bad Person, then you can see that it's an easy step to assume that bad things happening in your world must somehow be your fault. It's a bit like the spotlight phenomenon again, but this time, the spotlight is accusatory: *everything is bad and it's because of you!*

While engaging in personalizing, you might believe that everything others say or do is a direct personal reaction to you even when logically this doesn't fit. Personalizing directly impacts confidence; you cannot feel good about yourself if you feel that you are responsible for all the ills of the world around you. But then again, having low confidence primes you to dabble in a bit of personalizing. Hello—it's another vicious cycle.

As an example, think of your work colleague who walks into the office, stubs their toe, and proceeds to swear like a sailor. You instantly feel sheepish and apologize and can't shake the vague feeling that their anger is somehow directed at or about you. Without knowing why, you make it your personal mission to cheer them up for the rest of the afternoon. When we are unconfident, we can lack firm boundaries and get caught up in the emotions of others. To be confident, you have to be able to focus on yourself, not on the perceived reactions of others.

The opposite of personalizing is *externalizing*. It is another important cognitive distortion to note. When caught in this trap, individuals refuse to blame themselves for anything; instead, they blame everyone and everything else. These individuals blame others for holding them back and causing them pain or sadness, and even point to others as the cause of life's troubles. All of this blame is given without any recognition for the part that the individual played in his or her own troubles, pain, or sadness.

In order to escape from both of these cognitive distortions, question what part you actually played in the event and consider options in which you are not entirely to blame.

Were you truly the main actor in the event or did you just play a supporting role? If the blame was shifted to another actor, how might the event play out? Did you do the best you could? What were your intentions or motives? What would you change if you went back in time? How much of the situation could you truly control or influence?

By going through this mental rehearsal, you will be able to identify your true role in the event and the most likely person or thing that is actually at fault. More importantly, you'll gain a balanced view of situations so you can withstand them better.

"Marsha received a good education. Maybe she hasn't found a job that fulfills her yet. I did the best I could with what I knew at the time."

"Patricia didn't actually wait for us to arrive to serve the pot roast. Maybe our late arrival was just a coincidence. I have to admit, she has never been the best cook."

Overgeneralization

"I'm never going to find a girlfriend because my last date went so terribly. I am destined to be single forever."

"He will never be on time. He was late for both of our previous meetings. He's a lost cause. I am not going to meet with him again."

In the trap of *overgeneralization,* you take one or two negative experiences and assume all similar future experiences will be negative. Overgeneralization is unrepresentative of reality because you are operating on minimal experience, information, and evidence. You are jumping to conclusions and constructing a world that doesn't exist in reality, just in your limited exposure.

Common cues of overgeneralization are "always" and "never." When starting a sentence or a thought with "always" or "never," consider whether you have the experience or evidence to back up the statement. Do you have the ability to look past your current emotional feelings or the most recent event that is causing you to feel this way? The very nature of emotions is to overwhelm and cloud judgment—perhaps you are merely honoring your emotions instead of seeking a balanced view.

Overgeneralization is common in relationships and in the work environment. Often, past hurt or disappointment cloud your ability to envision a positive future.

To overcome the trap of overgeneralization, take time to question whether evidence may exist showing that future events could be different. Consider just how little information you have. Has every event of this type in your life ended in exactly the same way, or are there more than a few outliers? Do all of your friends have the exact same story, or have some of them had different experiences?

Would you feel differently when you're further removed from a situation and unemotional? Are you jumping to conclusions in a defensible way? If you believe that A + B = C, are A and B present, and is C a definite conclusion?

"Sure, Abby rejected me, but I've only been single for two months. Maybe I need a little more time to find someone more compatible."

"He was late for our two previous meetings, but there has been a lot of construction on Laurel Avenue. He might have just gotten caught up in the construction traffic last week."

Catastrophizing

"Lacy is out late again. I just know that she's cheating on me! We're never going to last as a couple; we have to be heading for divorce. I need to call a lawyer right now."

"Why haven't I received a letter from the University of California yet? They must be rejecting me. I can't believe it! I'm not going to get into any universities. What am I going to do? I guess I need to start learning how to become a plumber."

When you engage in *catastrophizing*, you immediately jump to the worst-case scenario and lose hope because the event seems so imminent. This is when you leap into an assumption with little to no evidence.

Confidence requires a belief that your actions can positively impact your future. By engaging in catastrophizing, you are limiting your ability to prepare for the future and take action to reach your goals.

Catastrophizing can cause you to become stressed and anxious. How confident can you really be if every day you appear to be facing your own personal version of the apocalypse?

As with other cognitive distortions, a degree of introspection and thinking about your thoughts is necessary. Question whether things are truly as bad as you are making them seem. Consider alternative explanations and past experiences in similar situations. What are the positive aspects of the event? In past similar situations, what did I do and how did the event turn out? How would an innocent bystander explain the situation? What am I fixating on and why? Perhaps most importantly, what does this say about me and my insecurities?

"Maybe Lacy is just working late; she mentioned a big work project when she was late last Wednesday. Oh, here's a text from her right now."

"The University of California said letters could arrive anytime this week. It's only Monday . . . Maybe a letter will come tomorrow."

Magnifying and Minimizing

"I'm so awful at writing legal briefs. Why can't I ever get this formatting right? I missed two punctuation errors in that fifty-page document. I'm trash."

"My puff pastry is the best of any of the chefs at Le Petit Poulet. My pastry cups are always perfectly formed and golden-brown. None of that matters. I'm still horrible."

Magnifying is choosing to focus on negative aspects of a situation or event until they seem to be the most important part. When engaging in the cognitive distortion of magnifying, you may focus on only parts of your body, aspects of your personality, or work traits that you view as negative while overlooking all of the other traits that are positive. Even if you've accomplished something great, you can't help but nitpick and see your victory in a negative light. It's as if you are wearing glasses that only allow you to see flaws and faults, no matter how small.

Minimizing is the opposite. This cognitive distortion occurs when you minimize positive events, aspects, or traits. While engaging in minimizing, you end up with the same view as when you magnify—nothing is good enough and you are inadequate. Take the same victory and you will downplay your accomplishments as unimportant and luck-based. You can do nothing right; it is mediocre at best. You might even minimize the present moment of positivity, choosing to focus on bleak events from the past, or a pessimistic forecast of the future.

You simply view yourself or your actions as flawed instead of taking a more realistic view. While engaging in the cognitive distortion of magnifying and minimizing, you ignore your positive attributes and fixate only on the negatives while doing the opposite for someone else. You may view your strengths in a way that makes them look inconsequential, while highly praising the same strengths of a coworker or friend. Both of these cognitive distortions cause you to view things in an unbalanced, unrealistic way.

To be confident, it is important to view the world realistically. By magnifying or minimizing negatives, your outlook becomes skewed and you are not able to make logical, well-considered decisions.

To overcome the trap of magnifying negativity,

challenge yourself to notice your positive attributes, list your strengths, and brainstorm reasons that you are deserving of praise or respect. Is this negative aspect a small detail or a large part of the event? What are some of the positive things about me or this event?

To overcome the cognitive distortion of minimizing positivity, do the same. Understand that you are capable and impactful.

"My formatting might not be perfect, but I always have the best phrasing and perfectly edited briefs. And really, I know my boss finds my formatting nicer than most of the other paralegals."

"I guess with how much everyone likes my pastry puffs and keeps asking for me personally, I'm doing something right. I'm not perfect, but there is plenty of real evidence that I am excelling."

Jumping to Conclusions

"Why didn't David smile back at me this morning? He must think the project proposal I sent him yesterday afternoon is stupid!"

"There's no point in even going to the gym. I'm never going to reach my goal of running that 10k with Candace."

Jumping to conclusions occurs when you make an irrational assumption about people or circumstances based on personal opinion and feeling. It begins with feelings of inadequacy or insecurity that influence the way you perceive events and statements. When you observe something that confirms your worst fears, you take it as a confirmation of everything you secretly knew to be terrible and true. Just like with other cognitive distortions, it causes you to fall down a rabbit hole of negativity until you end up at the worst possible conclusion.

There are two categories within the cognitive distortion of jumping to conclusions: mind-reading and fortune-telling.

While engaging in mind-reading, you assume you know what someone else is thinking. It is impossible to know exactly what someone else is thinking, yet with this cognitive distortion, people make decisions based on the imagined thoughts of other people. And of course, people are always thinking the worst about you.

Fortune-telling involves predicting negative future events without evidence. When engaging in fortune-telling, you predict only negative things for the future and have no real basis for doing so. Confident people understand the importance of being realistically optimistic; fortune-telling makes this impossible.

Building confidence for the future and taking steps toward reaching your goals require the ability to think realistically and plan specifically. You cannot be realistic or make useful plans if you are basing your thoughts off of hastily made conclusions.

To stop jumping to conclusions, question whether other explanations for events are possible or whether additional options exist. How else could you view this situation? If you believe in a certain conclusion, what are the pieces of evidence to support that? What other conclusions are more likely or common?

"David looked a little distracted. Maybe he didn't notice me smiling at him."

"If I go to the gym today, maybe I'll get a little closer to being ready to run the 10k. And if not, at least we can still switch to the 5k option."

Emotional Reasoning

"I can't afford to pay all of my bills again this month. I feel hopeless and depressed. There is no solution to my problems."

"Oh my gosh, why did I bring up that movie? It's ten years old; everyone will think I'm so out of touch. I'm such a bore at all these parties."

Engaging in the cognitive distortion of emotional reasoning means that you are taking your emotions as evidence. Whatever you feel right now is whatever reality you find yourself in. That's a difficult way to live.

While you're engaging in this behavior, observed evidence is discarded in favor of the "truth" of your feelings about the event. Humans tend to believe that how they feel must automatically be true. If you feel stupid and boring, then you must actually be stupid and boring. This is commonly referenced by the phrase: "I feel it; therefore, it must be true."

Emotional reasoning is one of the most dangerous of the cognitive distortions because it can be so wildly different from reality and in the span of minutes can change. Is reality actually changing moment by moment? Of course not! Only your emotions are changing that quickly.

Falling into the trap of emotional reasoning is different from the previously discussed skills of controlling your emotions and regulating how you choose to express them.

Being conscious of and allowing yourself to feel your emotions is important to maintaining your mental health and confidence; however, that does not mean that you should take your emotions to heart as a true expression of reality. In fact, your emotions often have very little to do with the status quo of reality. Remember, reality is neutral, yet your emotions cause you to perceive reality as either positive or negative. Many psychologists believe that emotional reasoning originates from negative thoughts and should be viewed as an uncontrolled or automatic response.

To escape the trap of emotional reasoning and take control of this "automatic response," question whether your emotional state of mind is preventing you from viewing events clearly. Just like you wouldn't go grocery shopping when hungry, you shouldn't evaluate anything when emotional. Always take time to return to a calm state before making decisions or committing yourself to a specific course of action. Do you feel bad about yourself or the situation at hand?

Viewing a situation while emotional, or with emotional reasoning, is like watching a completely neutral scene with horror music being played over it. And then joyous music. And then the next minute, music fitting for a clown's entrance. You won't know what's really happening in front of your face because the music will influence you a certain way. Finally, ensure that you are experiencing your emotions, but do not assume that your feelings are directly connected to reality.

"It is really upsetting to not have enough money, but that doesn't mean I can't find a solution. Maybe I should look into a side job. I know Maggie was talking about a great new tutoring client she found . . . I might be able to find a new client, too."

"That one statement might have been kind of boring. But I know that Mark thought our conversation about the new Korean restaurant was interesting. Just because I thought something I said was boring doesn't actually mean that everyone thinks I am boring."

Damaging Comparisons

Finally, although not a true cognitive distortion, viewing life through comparisons with others has the same tendency to create a negative reality.

Regardless of whatever strengths and qualities you bring to the table, you will become miserable when you compare yourself to others. We have a tendency to compare ourselves to other people around us or to some kind of imagined ideal—neither of these situations is good.

Comparing is a learned habit that destroys your confidence because it tries to put all your value and worth into one tiny aspect. You have to understand that you are a compilation of many different traits and talents. You have your looks, your earning ability, your ability to play sports, how fast you type, and so on. These all matter.

Unfortunately, when we compare ourselves to others, we ignore or throw out all the things we are good at and only focus on the one thing we're not good at or that we imagine others excel at. The problem with comparing in a social setting is that we often carry with us a fictionalized ideal of how a "perfect" person would get along in particular social situations.

This person is about as real as Superman. Unfortunately, we treat that notion as if it's absolutely real and we allow ourselves to feel crappy and inferior when we don't measure up. When we compare ourselves to this imagined ideal, we fail to see our strengths, value, and worth. If you keep doing this enough, your own confidence will take a permanent beating.

You will start off in any kind of social interaction with an automatic deficit. And this built-in inferiority complex compounds over time.

When you compare, you only see what's on the outside, what people allow others to see about them. But what you're seeing isn't the whole picture and is not necessarily who they really are—it's just their very best version of themselves; the one they are willing to present to the world. You end up degrading yourself by choosing your darkest and worst view of yourself to compare.

I repeat: you compare your *worst* moments to other people's *best* moments. What if that compelling public speaker nearly threw up before he delivered the speech that you were so impressed by?

When you come across somebody who seems to have their act together, always keep in the back of your mind that this person is not perfect. This person also has issues and insecurities like everyone else—like you. By always coming back to this central truth, you can throw some cold water on your natural tendency to elevate them and push yourself down.

Other people aren't only what they are showing to the world. Most people put on a good show. You probably know a couple who appears to get along great and are very much in love. They seem totally happy and to truly connect with each other in an enviable way. But do you really know what might be going on in their private life?

Take comfort from the fact that while there will be many people who are better at certain things than you are, there are also most certainly things that you will be better at. Keeping this in mind will enable you to have a more realistic set of expectations about yourself and others.

The next time you feel the compulsion to compare, ask yourself these three questions.

First, do I have all the information about this person?

The answer is almost certainly no.

Madonna might be an awesome performer and Taylor Swift may have a great stage presence, but that's just one aspect of the different traits that make them up as human beings. How can you possibly assume that one particular person is perfect when you don't have all the information about that person? Maybe that person you truly admire beats up their kids or is mean to their parents. Maybe that person has issues with substance abuse.

The answer is always the same. You don't have all the information about the other person, so why would you put them up on a pedestal? It's okay to put people up on a pedestal in terms of admiration, but never let that process result in your self-esteem taking a beating.

Second, are you judging yourself fairly?

Are you making a false comparison between someone's best and your worst, and letting emotion cloud your view of the situation? Are you using someone's success to make you feel like a failure, or is someone's success only so because of your failure?

Third, is this trait that you admire and are focused on really something that defines your own value as a person?

Are you falling into the trap of thinking that a particular trait or set of traits you're comparing to your own is what defines you as a person, and what you should draw your self-worth from?

For example, take Bill Gates. It's one thing to admire Bill Gates and his ability to spot an opportunity, create a winning company, and scale that vision up to benefit the lives of countless people all over the planet; it's another to look at Bill Gates's ability to make money as the crowning human trait that defines him as a person.

Imposter Syndrome and Its Cousin Perfectionism

One seldom considered cognitive distortion is the vague feeling that who we are is simply not enough somehow. This is not a true cognitive distortion but perhaps better understood as a culmination of several core beliefs, assumptions, and unchallenged ideas.

For example, you might be someone who lives under the constant shadow of an ideal image, the vision of the person you imagine you should be, could be—*must* be. This person is, for lack of a better word, perfect. While it's always good to have goals and dreams and to push ourselves, it can be taken too far if our imagined ideal is completely unrealistic.

This is why perfectionism and what's called imposter syndrome go hand in hand. We imagine some extremely idealistic self (perfectionism) and then we feel bad when we constantly compare ourselves to that image and find ourselves lacking—which of course we always will!

The problem is NOT that we are deficient or simply need to learn to be better. The problem is the goals we are setting and the expectations we are creating for our own performance.

Naturally, this then drains our confidence and leaves us feeling worthless. After all, no matter how good you are or how much you improve, you will never actually be flawless and perfect, so you will always look at your improvements as falling short. Isn't it crazy to set yourself a standard against which you *literally cannot* measure up?

Imposter syndrome shows up in professional contexts, but it can color an entire life. You get the creeping sensation that you don't really belong, that somehow all your accolades and achievements have been one happy accident, and that it's only a matter of time before you're discovered for the person you *really* are—a failure.

Even when you achieve or are praised for the good you do, you see this as evidence of how badly mistaken people are, and your anxiety ramps up because inside, you don't feel at all *worthy* of that praise, and feel even more dread that one day, you will be unmasked for who you really are.

We've already discussed the damage that all-or-nothing thinking can do, and it's not dissimilar for perfectionist thinking. Maybe some of us have been raised in families where striving for complete perfection is a question of control, or managing anxiety, or of proving to others that we are worth something.

But what does it say about our self-concept and our worth if we are only acceptable when we are one hundred percent perfect? Can you see how this is really just the core belief that, "I am so worthless and bad that only completely perfect performance will offset it"? In other words, at the heart of many people's perfectionism is the belief that they are worthless unless they are perfect.

This cognitive distortion may on the surface look like determination, hard work, and high standards, but in reality, it's fragile and unsustainable. Far healthier is the understanding that we don't have to be perfect to be worthy of attention, respect, happiness, or acknowledgement. Going even further, a solid sense of self isn't based on external appraisal at all—it comes from within us.

Acceptance Commitment Therapy (ACT)

So, if you've noticed some of these less-than-helpful cognitive distortions in yourself, what can be done about them? We've already discussed approaches for identifying and challenging harmful beliefs, as well as finding alternatives. However, it can be tricky to tease apart beliefs, thoughts, and feelings and differentiate them from character traits, coping mechanisms, or plain old bad habits.

ACT, or acceptance commitment therapy, helps you identify and overcome maladaptive patterns, whatever form they may take. Like many other approaches, it has foundations in mindfulness practice and is all about becoming *aware* of your negative thoughts and feeling patterns so you can *consciously* choose better ones. And, it's convenient that the acronym is ACT because that's precisely where your power comes from—making the commitment to actually **do** something about your situation.

It comes down to three main aspects:

1. Accept your reaction to things in the present moment
2. Choose a direction according to your own values and principles
3. Take inspired action

Let's take a closer look. First, what does it mean to accept ourselves just as we find ourselves in the moment? When we have low confidence, it's easy to be in a constant state of rejection or dismissal—we deny or hate how we feel, or we try to suppress or escape our thoughts and emotions. We obsess, worry, or judge ourselves. In short, we are *against ourselves*.

Acceptance means, conversely, that we are with ourselves. We might not like a situation or feeling, but we don't run away from it or ourselves. We don't push against what can't be changed, thereby making ourselves miserable. We simply embrace the peace that comes with accepting reality as it is.

Sounds nice and Zen, but it takes a lot of practice—sometimes a lifetime of practice! Actual mindfulness practice or meditation can help strengthen our ability to simply observe what arises in us without needing to cling, reject, analyze, or interpret it. But there are other strategies to increasing acceptance in yourself.

For example, remind yourself often that you don't need to be perfect. Think of the people you love and how you love them despite (or even because of?) their flaws. Every time your attention goes to something you dislike in yourself, consciously choose to balance it out by thinking of something you *do* like. Notice that you are a complete and complex person— someone who is who they are, with good and bad attributes, and all of it's okay.

Think of your life like an interesting novel— and those character flaws, bad events, or mistakes are all a vital part of the unfolding plot, and add color and dimension. Realize that *you don't have to act on feelings and thoughts* that arise inside you—you can simply be there, watch them come, and then watch them go again.

Even feeling insecure, worthless, unconfident, or anxious is in itself nothing to be worried about. Can you look at even these feelings and say, "Well, I feel how I feel, and I'm okay. I have permission to be a flawed human being and a work in progress. I choose to stay present here with myself even through difficulty"?

Here is the magic, of course: you always are in control of how you react to spontaneous and emerging feelings. For example, you may not have much control over a knee-jerk emotional reaction that was programmed into you long ago when you were a child. You cannot do much about your shortcomings or mistakes you've legitimately made. But you *can* decide what you will do in response to all this. In other words, you can choose your own direction now, out of the present moment. Once you become aware of the vehicle that is the present, you can take charge and steer it according to what you most value. You can only do this when you have done the first step, however, which is to actually acknowledge and accept where you really are.

The final step is then to act in accordance with what you are consciously choosing for yourself. You can act to change the situation, or you can act to continue it, appreciate it, or merely tolerate it. It is also a choice to not do anything, if that feels right. The big idea, however, is that it is you who is *choosing to act* from conscious deliberation and not from unconscious habit and unthinking emotional reaction.

Think about someone who considers themselves unconfident. They're navigating the dating process and are feeling unworthy and inexperienced, petrified of what others will think of them, and apprehensive that they will be painfully rejected and forever alone.

According to ACT, their first step is to accept. There's no need for hot-air and pep talks in the mirror (who really believes all those positive affirmations or well-meaning compliments from Mom?). Instead, they could stop and become aware. Observe what they are feeling. Notice their body sensations, their emotions, their thoughts, and how they are speaking to themselves internally.

Maybe they notice they feel nauseous and shaky, like they're about to shatter or melt, and that their mind is filled with thoughts like,

This is so humiliating.

You're old and ugly and fat. Nobody wants you.

This date is not going to go well. I can just feel it . . .

When we accept our current state, we gain distance. We are able to acknowledge our thoughts and feelings *as thoughts and feelings*—i.e. we are no longer wrapped up in them, wholly identifying with them as though they are reality itself. We can see that we are simply having an experience. It's not plain fact or an unending reality, but an interpretation of a transient sensation. This alone makes things more manageable.

Let's say the person takes a step back and notices that this is how they are in the moment, and they consciously choose to say, "That's okay. You're having negative thoughts and feelings right now, which will pass. You're engaging in cognitive distortions, and you're running into automatic thoughts that are causing you to see things as worse than they probably are."

Now is the key moment—do they want to continue down this path? They have the choice.

Either by sitting down with a journal, doing a breathing exercise, or simply spending some time in contemplation, the person might come to realize that they want to steer things in a different direction. They want to feel better about themselves and more at ease with who they are. They are nervous, yes, but they have other good qualities—good humor, kindness, etc.—that they want to focus on right now.

The final step is to act. None of the above means anything if it stays theoretical and nothing changes. The person needs to accept where they are, identify an alternative path, and then *actively choose that path*—it's a question of commitment, which takes courage and boldness.

Seeing where they are internally and deciding that they would like to behave differently, the person in our example then commits to making that alternative a reality. Maybe they ask a friend to look over their online dating profile to make sure they're not selling themselves short. Maybe they commit to going out that evening and set the target of speaking to one person, any person, simply for the sake of practicing social chit chat. Maybe their confidence-boosting act is to set a boundary and actually say no to a dating prospect that a more unconfident person would tolerate. Whatever it is, the action part of the equation needs to concretely move you forward and play out in the real world.

If you know about CBT, mindfulness-based practices, or other self-help techniques, the principles of ACT will seem familiar to you. The difference with ACT, however, is that we consciously choose to take awareness and self-compassion and use it to drive real action in our lives. The key is that action comes from acceptance and an acknowledgement of alternatives. Without them, action is just action and means nothing. But if action is inspired by our genuine self-awareness and acceptance, it has the potential to actually spur change.

Here's the process summarized. If you notice you're in a distressed or overwhelmed state, pause and ask yourself these questions in order:

1. What is my current experience in this moment, and how can I accept it?

2. What are my deepest values and goals? And how can I use those to guide how I direct and steer this moment?

3. What is the single next concrete action I can take in that direction?

Here's an example from someone who has just received negative feedback from a superior at work:

1. I am feeling ashamed, embarrassed, exposed, uncomfortable, tearful. I can take a moment to head to the washroom and sit quietly by myself for a moment, just to find my breath and composure. I know that criticism sets off my negative self-talk, but I will just sit with it and watch it. I don't have to *believe* it. My self-talk is all or nothing: either you're perfect or you're a loser. I see that this is not rational, though.

2. I know that being criticized is not the end of the world. I want to be a person who is resilient and open to feedback, and who can learn from mistakes. I can be a hard worker *and* mess up sometimes. But to be that, I need to steer this moment in a different direction. I accept that I feel bad about it all, but I feel better when I know I can choose where to go from here.

3. I choose to take a deep breath, to thank my supervisor for the feedback, and to write down several concrete ways to make sure I'm better in the future. In

fact, I will immediately take action right now to make right on some work I submitted previously.

By using methods like ACT, restructuring our core beliefs or deliberately challenging cognitive distortions, we are making attempts to rewire our brain's functioning and ultimately change how we feel, think, and behave in the world. It's like digging down in the code of a piece of software and painstakingly rewriting the buggy bits. But once that's done, hopefully the program runs more smoothly.

Once healthier, more rational core beliefs are in place and once you make consistent efforts to return to them in favor of dwelling on the old programming, your new thought patterns will become more and more automatic and natural feeling. You won't have to sit down with a journal for twenty minutes to dissect the best way to respond—you'll just respond.

Your self-talk emerges from these internal programs, and once you change the programs, your self-talk changes accordingly. We'll look at self-talk and how to deliberately rework it in the next section.

Transform Your Self-Talk

Cognitive Behavior Therapy (CBT) is an effective framework for organizing attempts to reprogram your self-talk thought by thought. It's typically practiced with a psychotherapist or counselor, but the principles are accessible and can be applied on your own—in fact, some of the exercises in the previous sections have been informal examples of CBT exercises.

CBT can address a whole range of life problems, but is particularly suited for understanding and changing underlying core beliefs in a systematic way. CBT techniques help you identify and take control of certain mental processes, cope with stress and adversity, resolve conflicts, and deal with grief, illness, trauma, and more. When practiced regularly, CBT can also induce changes in brain chemistry that were once thought possible only through medication. As such, improvements that result from CBT are highly likely to be long lasting, since they can fundamentally alter the way our minds function.

While the risks associated with CBT are minimal, it's worth being prepared to face some potentially uncomfortable feelings, or confront difficult beliefs and fears. Most importantly, CBT won't magically make life's problems go away. Rather, it will teach you to better cope with them and to face challenges with empowered autonomy and the self-confidence needed to cope and thrive.

CBT doesn't always work (and it's okay if it doesn't!), but you can improve your chances of success by:

- Opting to work with a counselor or at least sharing your journey with someone you trust.

- Being willing to be open and honest with yourself—embarrassment and denial will only get in the way.

- Being dedicated. We may be convinced that our own case is hopeless and beyond repair, but CBT takes time and consistent effort to work. Bear in mind that there are no miraculous overnight results, and half-hearted attempts here and there are unlikely to have lasting effects.

Three-Step Cognitive Behavioral Therapy

CBT is evidence-based and well-suited to tackling the inner dialogue that accompanies worry, anxiety, regret, shame, grief, guilt, blame, and low self-esteem. Life is filled with challenges, adversities, and unexpected events.

These can either be viewed as painful and unfair, or manageable and growth-inspiring—all depending on the mindset we cultivate with our self-talk.

CBT is not about "thinking positively" but thinking more clearly, realistically, and neutrally—without cognitive distortions. In CBT, our thoughts, feelings, and behavior are all interconnected, i.e. if we can change our thoughts, we can change our feelings and consequently how we act (and vice versa).

We've covered some cognitive distortions already—catastrophizing, black-and-white thinking, etc.—and have begun recognizing the language of negative self-talk in ourselves. Observing your thinking and becoming aware of previously automatic thoughts and distortions is step 1.

Step 2 is learning to gently and consistently challenge these thoughts and their underlying core beliefs, testing just how accurate they are. We considered this in the previous chapter where we asked ourselves questions, tested our assumptions, and encouraged ourselves to seek alternatives.

Step 3 is doing the work of replacing these distorted thoughts and beliefs with ones that are healthier, more accurate, and more likely to lead to a balanced and optimistic life. Before we move on to this very important step, however, we need to look a little closer at the language of negative self-talk and how to spot triggers and warning signs so that we can step in and stop cognitive distortions *before* they take flight in our minds.

Step 1: Observe

Self-talk is made of words. That's all it is.

It's literally like a film script that you run internally. But words can be edited, deleted, rewritten. In previous sections, we've focused on fact versus fiction and the importance of comparing our thoughts against objective reality as much as possible. This is a way of fine-tuning the *content* of our thoughts, but there's also the question of the style, grammar, vocabulary, and tone of the language we use when we talk to ourselves.

You've utterly failed, you big fat idiot.

You didn't pass the quiz that time.

Both of these statements can refer to the same event, and in a way are factually equivalent— i.e. "didn't pass" is the same as "failed." However, it's obvious that they carry very different emotional nuances and will have very different effects on the person thinking them.

Automatic negative self-talk has a certain flavor that you can recognize with practice. It's usually short, spontaneous, and emotionally loaded with strong words, or has a rambling, looping quality. It's filled with overgeneralizing language like *always*, *never*, *nobody*, *should*, *nothing*, *must*, and *completely*, or language filled with guilt, self-flagellation, and judgment.

Watch for language that spirals or feeds on itself or steadily mounts in intensity. Look out for thoughts that you accept as true immediately in the moment without a second thought. Automatic thoughts are usually strongly infused with feelings of fear, anger, or shame, and will appear in language that suggests this—at the very least, you'll know it's negative self-talk simply because you feel awful when you listen to it!

Step 2: Challenge

If you catch yourself in negative self-talk—congratulations. Even better, however, would be to avoid it altogether or stop it before it happens using your knowledge of what usually triggers these thoughts for you. Negative thoughts are easier to recognize and handle when they are still small.

As a technique, "thought stopping" appeared in the late 1950s in the sport psychology world, and was used to cut short self-defeating and anxious thoughts that got in the way of performance. An excellent overview can be found in Zinsser, Bunker, and Williams' 2010 book, *Cognitive Techniques for Building Confidence and Enhancing Performance*. The idea is to use a behavioral or mental cue to snap out of a negative self-talk spiral.

For those suffering from mental health issues like panic disorders, it can be especially hard to distract yourself once a negative thought appears in your mind. This technique acts as a tool to help become aware of and then replace these thoughts in a way similar to practicing mindfulness.

Pinching yourself, imagining a red light, or saying "stop" out loud can all act as cues to bring your conscious awareness to the moment and away from negative self-talk.

It's essentially the art of beneficial distraction, and even more effective when you then quickly redirect your attention to a preferable subject (a more realistic thought, perhaps?). It's an assertive stance you are taking against that inner dialogue that you know only carries you to places you don't want to go.

The technique can potentially backfire if you end up constantly monitoring yourself to look for failures you can pounce on—the trick is to bring mindfulness to the process, not punishment or judgment. If you try this technique for a while and find it actually worsens the problem, ease up, be more compassionate, or simply attempt a different technique. Thought stopping may help for more superficial rumination, but not for deeper anxieties that may respond better to slow, deliberate engagement.

If you'd like to try the technique, however, here's how to begin:

Write down a list of all the most distressing, recurring, distracting, and unwanted thoughts you wish to stop paying attention to. Try to rank them from most to least distressing. Include anything from, "One day my boss is going to figure out how inept I am and fire me," to, "This lump probably means cancer."

Next, do some prep work by practicing—sit alone in a private room and spend some time visualizing any situation in life where the most distressing thought might conceivably intrude. For a while, go into the thought and focus on it, feeling out its contours. Then, as abruptly as you can, stop the thought.

Stand up quickly, say "Stop!" out loud, snap your eyes open, make a loud clapping noise, or click your fingers. Empty your mind and try to hold that emptiness for thirty seconds or so. If the thought tries to intrude again, repeat "stop" as often as necessary.

What you are trying to do is gain practice at stopping rumination mid-thought. In time you can be less drastic with your interruption and eventually internalize the "stop" so you only say it quietly to yourself. You don't necessarily need to use the word *stop*—you could also visualize your thoughts as traffic that stops dutifully at a red light. Try saying out loud, "I'm having a thought about XYZ right now," to remind yourself that it's just a thought, and to gain distance.

Whatever you do, simply remind yourself that thoughts are just words—just a script that you can stop in its tracks and rewrite. The hard work is to recognize the thought, but once you do, realize it has no hold on you unless you pay attention to it. Make a habit of using certain phrases to interrupt unwanted thoughts, divert your attention, and affirm your *choice* to follow certain thoughts and drop others:

Don't go there

Let it be

Let it go

It's in the past

Leave it alone

Focus

Don't pay attention

Slow down

This, too, will pass

It doesn't matter

Breathe

You've got this

Using this thought-stopping technique may make some people uncomfortable—aren't you just ignoring your problems?

It's worth remembering that thought stopping is best used for those thoughts that you know are intrusive, unwanted, and genuinely unhelpful. These are the thoughts that you have already identified as irrational, untrue, or exaggerated, and you know that entertaining them will only lead to stress and worry.

Your goal is to tolerate and manage anxiety rather than turn a blind eye to it. Similarly, having thought stopping in your mental toolkit doesn't mean you are unable to hear your own intuition or engage when a situation warrants genuine concern. Thought stopping is merely a mental fuse that lets you halt catastrophic rumination before you get too carried away with it.

For some people, the thought-stopping technique outlined above may feel a little punitive and may not work for them. Thankfully, there are plenty of other techniques underpinned by the same principles. You could try scattered counting, for example. Counting to ten is a common anger-management technique, but it's easy enough to become automatic, allowing your brain to carry on ruminating even as you count. Rather, jump around with random numbers to engage your thoughts more, e.g. "43, 12, 5, 88, 356, 90, 5 . . ."

In the same way, a mantra or spoken word can interrupt runaway thoughts—choose a more complicated nonsense phrase or something in another language to prevent yourself from doing it too automatically. Alternatively, you can select affirmations based on your specific triggers or perceived negative qualities. Though they can take time to work, the reason so many find them effective is that our brains eventually come to think of them as true. These affirmations can be specific quotes from religious texts, or statements like, "I believe in myself," and, "I am in charge of my thoughts." These can be recited both mentally and out loud, but with conviction. Repeating lines you don't really believe will be pointless, so choose your affirmations wisely.

You could try self-soothing with encouraging positive self-talk, such as: "Don't worry, you can handle this," or, "You're doing great!" Play a song you like or listen to a podcast to engage your auditory channels and pull attention away from anxious overthinking.

A distracting cue can also be physical in nature—physically move yourself into a different position, get up and do a few jumping jacks, or go for a quick jog outside to break out of thought loops. You can also switch to more bodily/somatic awareness by simply focusing on your breath and practicing a technique called muscle isolation.

Sit or lie comfortably, close your eyes, and then work your way through all your muscles, starting from the ones in your toes. Squeeze them as tightly as you can for five seconds and then release and relax completely. Then focus on the muscles in your feet and legs, moving up until you reach the muscles in your face and scalp. Not only will this help immensely to release physical tension, but it will distract your overactive mind and bring it more fully into the present moment.

Muscle isolation can be an excellent warmup to a more formal sitting meditation practice, or a great way to end a mindfulness session. Combine it with gentle soothing music or head outside where you can feel the sun and breeze on your skin.

Another classic CBT technique is to decide that instead of stopping or running away from scary and overwhelming thoughts, you'll simply stare them down and ask what's the worst that could happen. Look squarely at your ruminations and say, *so what?* It's rarely as bad as you think, and seldom something you truly cannot handle. Research has found that even those who lose their limbs or eyesight—suffering tragedies anyone would consider horrifying—soon return to a median level of happiness because of how powerful our modes of adaptation are. As such, no matter what it is you're worried over, you're very likely to be able to survive it just fine even if the event were to occur.

You might like to visualize yourself actually encountering the worst-case scenario with grace and poise, tackling the problem and seeing that it isn't in fact the end of the world, even if the worst does come to pass. This alone can take the steam out of your most catastrophic ruminations.

Step 3: Replace

Some thoughts are so useless and untrue that they can be discarded immediately or stopped using any of the techniques described above. With practice, you'll be able to recognize totally harmful thoughts (like, "I'm probably going to die," or, "Everyone hates me") and release them immediately.

Some ideas and thoughts, however, are a little more subtle and are more appropriately rewritten rather than discarded entirely. These thoughts are often those that we believe have a grain of truth to them. Here, it's necessary to practice a degree of conscious discernment to determine what kind of life script will serve you best. Again, this is a step that can only be done *after* you've gained a good awareness of the kinds of self-talk you engage in—otherwise, you risk having these techniques exacerbate rather than solve the problem.

Exercise 1: Think it through

This exercise takes some time and effort. The first step is to note down your self-talk using any of the methods already discussed (for example, by using a bullet journal, writing down your core beliefs, or periodically taking a self-esteem inventory). Then, after a week, try to look for particular themes or patterns.

What kind of self-talk is it (for example, catastrophizing or mindreading)?

What events, thoughts, feelings, people, or situations triggered the self-talk?

What common threads can you identify?

What was the effect or result of these thoughts?

What do they say about your core beliefs?

Reflect on what you see. Get some distance on your thoughts. This way, we're more likely to evaluate them truthfully, as opposed to in the moment when our feelings might cloud our judgement. Notice if your self-talk has actually held you back in life or made you feel bad. Ask yourself how it would feel to have positive self-talk instead. What might your life look like and what could you achieve if you didn't limit yourself in this way?

In thinking through things carefully, the more positive alternative is likely to appear to you. For example, you may see that you constantly exaggerate physical symptoms and then get stuck in doom-and-gloom thought loops about what might happen if you fall ill. Seeing all this objectively noted on paper, seeing how it negatively impacts your life in many ways, and seeing how utterly irrational it is, you slowly begin to loosen the self-talk's hold on you.

By completing this exercise, you can begin to see the more accurate and realistic options available to you. Better yet, when you try them out and monitor yourself for a week, you may be surprised to learn just how much wasted mental energy and anguish you can avoid by consciously and deliberately dropping negative self-talk.

Takeaways:

- What is a cognitive distortion? It is a pattern of thinking that is unrepresentative of reality. This is significant because most cognitive distortions are disempowering and cause you to doubt yourself, lose confidence, and lose mental toughness. How can you be mentally tough if the world seems to be pitted against you? You're just starting from a place where you can't win.
- Cognitive distortions are often automatic thought patterns that arise from our own insecurities and fears. They aren't totally unfounded, but they depart wildly from

reality. They are characterized by jumping to conclusions based on assumptions and incomplete information, as well as overreactions.

- A few of the most well-known and dangerous cognitive distortions are all-or-nothing thinking, personalizing, overgeneralizing, catastrophizing, magnifying and minimizing, and jumping to conclusions. An especially notable cognitive distortion that robs us of resilience is emotional reasoning. This is when reality is defined by the emotions we feel at that very moment. Another is perfectionism, which can often lead to us *never* feeling adequate and the phenomenon of imposter syndrome.

- Comparisons are not necessarily a cognitive distortion, but they create the same skewed reality and set of expectations. You should evaluate yourself according to your own baseline, instead of comparing your worst to other people's best.

- Acceptance commitment therapy (ACT) is a simple but powerful approach where we convert our awareness of our own thought patterns into concrete action. We learn to be aware of and accept how we feel, and then we consciously choose the direction we want to take instead according to our values. Finally, we take action, no matter

how small, in that direction. We don't *have
to* act on negative thoughts and feelings!

Chapter 4. The Importance of Action (. . . and Exactly How to do It)

The previous two chapters were about addressing your thoughts and slowly but surely altering them through various cognitive techniques. This is a process that works for many because it literally changes the way you think. Imagine the power of shedding your current assumptions about your relationships with people, and reprogramming all your negative thoughts with carefree ones.

However, there is a drawback to this approach. It's slow. It's hard. It's a process where you can take two steps forward only to take one step back. It can take months or years because you are completely reversing and substituting thought patterns you've had since you were a child. If you have low self-confidence, the temptation to self-chastise may be strong, especially if you have a few setbacks along the way.

CBT attempts to apply logic to emotion. That's a tall charge because even though you logically know what you should be doing, your emotions can prevent you from acting on it—remember all that stuff about the amygdala? That leap from emotion to logic doesn't always happen. You *logically* know you should stop watching television and do your homework. Makes no difference, does it? So contrary to what others would have you believe, we can't always *logic* confidence into existence. Fear is not logical, and you can't reason with it. It doesn't listen to your arguments, nor does it have any interest in making sacrifices for the greater good.

Again, it's not to say that CBT isn't one of the most effective weapons against a lack of confidence, but we do have another option. As we've already seen with the technique of ACT, confidence can be built through the life-changing magic of *doing*, taking action, making a leap of faith, closing your eyes and walking forward, and going for it. Action is the magic missing link.

Stop thinking and planning and instead get firsthand experience. *Prove* to yourself that your distortions and assumptions are bogus. Take a leap sooner rather than later. (Of course, this is best used simultaneously with some form of CBT and challenging your core beliefs.)

Instead of talking and analyzing until you feel better about yourself to act, action takes the opposite route. Jump into the deep end (within reason), survive (because you inevitably will), and you will feel your confidence grow from your experiences. No matter how much CBT you've used on yourself, there is likely never a point where you actually feel comfortable, ready, and confident, but that's just the thing. You can't wait until you feel like you have built up all your confidence, because that moment will never come. You'll be stuck waiting forever. In a way, it's our old friends perfectionism and black-and-white thinking rearing their ugly heads again. Taking action first takes care of all this.

For instance, if you want to attempt skydiving, then at some point, sooner or later, you just have to jump. There's no amount of rumination or preparation that will truly make you feel confident in jumping out of a flying piece of metal with only a parachute strapped to your back. And no amount of logic or rationalization is going to lessen the fear you feel. But once you jump and land safely, you truly know what you feared will do you little to no harm. And that's a realization that confidence can grow from.

Understand that confidence actually *follows* action, not the opposite. When we think about confidence, we want something that will light a spark in us and make us feel invincible. We want *confidence that causes action*. There are a few problems with this, namely the fact that you're probably looking for something that doesn't exist, and that's going to keep you waiting on the sidelines, out of action and out of the race.

The truth is you should plan for life *without* a confidence kickstart. Have you ever heard the expression that courage is feeling fear and doing it anyway? The fact is that the fear is there, so we might as well face it. Seeking that confidence before we can act creates a prerequisite and additional barrier to living your life. It can become an excuse. Instead, get into the habit of proceeding without it. Expect that you have to leap out of that airplane eventually, and it will get easier the more you practice. And surprisingly, this is where you'll find what you were seeking. *Action leads to confidence.* For repetition's sake, forget confidence; get started and you'll *become* confident.

A taste of action tells you that everything will be okay and you have nothing to fear. This is confidence rooted in firsthand experience, which is easier to find as opposed to false confidence you get from trying to convince yourself before the fact that you can do it—no matter how effective and thorough your CBT can be.

Public speaking is almost always a scary proposition. Consider how you might try to find confidence that causes action: you would tell yourself it will all be fine, imagine the audience in their underwear, and remind yourself of your hours of rehearsal. Is that convincing?

Now consider how you might find confidence *after* getting started—after seeing how the audience reacts to you, after hearing the applause, and most importantly, after seeing that your worst nightmare did not come true. "I *did* it and it *was* fine," is a strong argument for confidence versus: "I haven't done it yet, but I *think* it will be fine."

The most important takeaway here is to not wait until you are one hundred percent ready before you take the first step. If you're anywhere above a sixty percent (give or take ten percent) level of confidence, then it's already time to act. Only through starting down the road will you build your confidence up to that elusive one hundred percent mark. Change your expectations regarding confidence and remove the self-imposed requirements you have for yourself.

Confidence typically only exists inside your

comfort zone. The reason you are reading this book is your comfort zone is too small, so you feel anxious more than you'd like. You have to continually take steps outside of your comfort zone to keep expanding it, or you'll be right where you started. As with CBT, it can be a slow process—as the saying goes, if you keep doing what you've been doing, you'll keep getting the results you've been getting—whereas three seconds of fearlessness can be like using dynamite to expand your comfort zone.

What about the prospect of failure? This may sound counterintuitive, but failure is one of the best things that can happen to you. Failure is one of the best teachers you will ever have in your life, and its value will far exceed any successes you have. We successfully learn what not to do when we fail, and eventually, knowing what not to do becomes as valuable as knowing what *to* do.

Sadly, when we spend so much time and energy trying to evade and avoid failure, we end up learning those hard lessons later on. Instead of trying to avoid failure, look at it straight in the eye, learn what you need to learn, and move on. Don't spend your time trying to stay afloat just to avoid failure. That just leads to half-measures and won't teach you much about yourself.

For example, meticulously pick apart why you failed in a specific social situation and exactly what caused your confidence to tank or otherwise not rise. Attempt to understand what you did wrong, what you did right, and what was special regarding the situation. You can then use this information so you can avoid making that same mistake in the future.

Come up with a pattern or theory of why things fell apart and what the solution is. Test your solution by practicing again and again with other groups of people. By embracing failure and divorcing it from feelings of alienation, regret, shame, and embarrassment, you can make great progress.

We have been programmed since early on to read all sorts of mental and emotional judgments into failure. Just because you failed doesn't mean you are less of a person. Don't let failure lead to an emotional shutdown that gives you anxiety or frustrates you. It's just feedback that something was out of place, and a veritable blueprint on how to succeed next time.

The problem with success is that you don't know which part of the experience produced the positive result. With failure, it's easier to break apart your actions and understand the patterns that lead to disappointment, discouragement, and frustration. Failure can be a steppingstone to greater success if you let it fulfill that role.

Your level of confidence is a reflection of your relationship with failure. Most people are so afraid of *doing and failing* that it erodes their level of confidence and prevents them from ever attempting the doing again. Unfortunately, the true, straightforward, and direct path to building confidence begins with doing, which will occasionally end in failure. The key is to do more, reduce failure, then repeat the process again.

Try an experiment if you dare: head out into the world and attempt something new with the deliberate intention that you will fail at it. Instead of reaching some arbitrary perfect objective, make your only goal one of action and of tolerating failure. Know that you'll fail, do it anyway, and see for yourself that the world doesn't end. In fact, your action and subsequent failure provide you with enormous amounts of useful information and learning if you can prevent your ego or anxiety from distorting everything.

Deliberately pick up a book that's too difficult for you, chat up a person you know will reject you, or attempt a project that you know you don't have the skills for. Well, you already know that failure is imminent, so, in a way, you can relax! A funny thing might happen, though. You may realize that failure is only painful when combined with a particular set of interpretations and beliefs. With a different set, it just becomes a boring, possibly even useful, part of everyday life. And it's something you *can* survive. The next time you approach a similar situation, you'll feel more at ease because what's the worst that could happen? Congratulations—this feeling is none other than confidence. And it's a confidence you would not have found without taking that vital step of action.

We've hammered home the point that action is equally as important as changing your toxic thoughts. Confidence follows action, and a dash of fearlessness is often more effective than slowly building confidence. So what is the actual action we should be taking?

The thrust of how to actually take action is exposure therapy and creating a fear hierarchy specific to confidence. There is one intermediate step, however, that you can take—take care of the low-hanging fruit. These are the most common insecurities associated with a lack of confidence.

Most people have a relatively clear idea about the sources of their insecurity. You might feel that you don't dress well, you stutter when you speak, and you can't approach new people. Even having a rough idea of your insecurities can be important. It's time to start doing something about that—actively—and tackle the low-hanging fruit to minimize sources of your insecurity.

Even if you start with a hundred insecurities and manage to eliminate only one, that's one less thing you have to worry about. The longer you choose not to resolve or work on your insecurities, the longer your insecurities will continue to drag you down. Don't get stuck in self-pity thinking about your lack of confidence; be proactive and solution oriented. Rather than ask you to articulate the Pandora's Box of your biggest social insecurities, I have two ways for you to minimize your insecurities, starting one by one. If you can adequately address the next two points, confidence immediately becomes more tangible and reachable. In fact, they might be all that's necessary for you to gain momentum toward true confidence.

You are insecure about your appearance.

You might think that making a drastic effort here is pandering to people, but that's just the way the world works. My apologies.

People do judge books by their covers. You can

complain and whine all you want about how this should not be the case—but hey, living in reality is all about focusing on how things actually are and not obsessing about how things should be. While you can try to change people's minds and assumptions, you still have to deal with the reality on the ground.

You feel that your appearance is getting in the way of your confidence. There's no way around it. You are either not feeling good about yourself and it shows, or you are dressing and carrying yourself in a way that causes other people to pre-judge you—which we know creates a lukewarm reception that you will probably notice.

Luckily, this is the easiest category to change. It's about carrying yourself with better posture and asking a friend of the opposite sex how they would groom and dress you better. When you look good, you feel good, and other people feel good about being around someone that feels good. Did you get that?

At first, it might feel as if you're wearing a costume. But hey—the old you wasn't doing your confidence any favors, was it? The bottom line is to just give a damn about this and realize that it's a huge part of the equation—one that others seem to naturally manage. It's actually highly manufactured with lots of effort.

Sometimes change can start from the outside in, just like sometimes confidence can come *after* action.

You are insecure about running out of things to say or saying something stupid.

If you are self-conscious and worried that people will judge you if you say something stupid or "off," there's an easy workaround to that.

The best approach is simple preparation. Create answers to predictable questions and conversations. Run that mental videotape in your mind about your past ten, twenty, or thirty social conversations. I guarantee they are not all that different from each other.

All social conversations, especially among total strangers, tend to follow certain predictable patterns. It's very, very rare that you will have a really deep, profound, existential, and philosophically rich conversation with somebody you don't know from Adam.

While it does happen, those conversations are rare pieces of brain candy. For the most part, our social conversations tend to be fairly shallow. Use this to your advantage.

Since you know there are only so many

directions a typical conversation in a light social setting will take, be proactive. Figure out the general questions that people will ask and the topics that will come up in normal conversation and be prepared with story-answers.

For example,

How was your weekend?
What are you doing this weekend?
How was your day?
What do you do for work?

The key is to realize that these questions are just people's attempts to hear something interesting and not actually requests for literal, mundane answers. You can think about these beforehand, and simply by being prepared, you will freak out less.

Instead of feeling intimidated and scared, by thinking through these kinds of questions and your answers ahead of time, you gain confidence knowing that you will perform well because you have rehearsed your answers.

Predictability is the foundation to social comfort. If you want to be comfortable in any kind of social setting, even if you are dealing with complete and total strangers, look for predictable patterns. But the crux of this chapter and taking action toward confidence in general is exposure therapy.

Exposure Therapy

This is really where the rubber meets the road regarding taking action. With almost anyone suffering through some kind of fear, the first line of defense is simple: avoidance. Keep away from the situation or thing that's the object of your fears. The agoraphobic just has to stay away from heights. Arachnophobes do all they can to keep spiders out of sight. Those with low confidence avoid anything that drives home the feeling that they suck—presentations, work evaluations, or being put on the spot in a group conversation. It's not a perfect strategy, but it can work to a certain extent.

Avoidance is the primary shield for those without confidence as well, but it's not always possible (nor recommendable) to maintain total isolation from the rest of society. At some point, they're going to have to mix in with the public, at least if you want to eat, earn a livelihood, and have any semblance of friendships or relationships.

Many would simply advise the social phobic to go all in and just thrust themselves into public without too much thought. It's often proposed that you should dive into the deep end of the pool and simply stop overthinking. It's a strategy, to be sure, but it's also like telling someone to simply be taller. It feels like an impossible ask—no phobic can approach what they're scared of without thought, and lots of it. Placing someone with no confidence into social anarchy would only accelerate their sense of panic and cause more mortal dread, kind of like a person thrown into the deep end may panic and drown just because it's too overwhelming.

Instead, a more guided, gradual, and consistent approach might be the answer: *situational exposure, also known as exposure therapy.* This tactic allows for a progressive, deliberate, controlled introduction into the social world and gaining confidence. You'll have the opportunity to dismantle your anxieties with baby steps by remaining in a social setting just long enough to settle your anxieties. You'll have more time to adapt to the situation and your body will react more gently than if you were thrown in the deep end. With each step in exposure therapy, you'll advance your self-reliance and confidence. What's important, though, is that with each step, you are taking meaningful action and getting closer to being the kind of person you want to be.

The working principle behind exposure therapy is that when you force yourself to stay in the situation and fully experience the range of emotions you feel in that moment—be it discomfort, anger, anxiety, or fear—you'll come to find those difficult emotions easier and easier to tolerate and accept. You can only manage them successfully if you've reached a point where you're comfortable enough to stay with the difficult emotions it may elicit, and that can only happen when you stop evading it every time it crops up.

In essence, you find that things are not as bad as you thought they were, and you survived just fine. This allows fears and anxieties to slowly die down through the realization that negative consequences won't follow. It's like how vaccinations work: you inject yourself with a small amount of something that your body can easily handle, and then you are prepared for more powerful versions of the same sickness.

As you gradually expose yourself to more and more challenging scenarios, you also build a higher and higher tolerance for the discomfort from a lack of confidence.

Just imagine how you would learn to swim. You would first learn in a shallow pool where you can reach the bottom. Then after some time, you might graduate to floating in a deeper pool, but with a floating board. Then, you might ditch the board and learn to put your head underwater. Overcoming something scary will always take steps, because that's how our minds are programmed to accept and feel comfort. You could jump directly into the ocean, and some people *can* learn that way, but most of us will drown.

It's a process that gently allows you firsthand experience into feelings of safety and security while pushing the envelope until you're at the point you wanted. For everyone who shies away from taking action once the time is finally here, exposure therapy makes action so easy that it almost doesn't feel like anything is being accomplished until you consider in hindsight.

How does the process work for gaining confidence in particular? How can we ease ourselves into confidence little by little?

1. List the situations you avoid. Ask yourself what kinds of gatherings or circumstances you steer clear of and write them all down in a list. Your list should include both physical situations—parties, family gatherings, work presentations, and so forth—*and* personal experiences that you don't want to face.

For example, you might have an aversion to being the focal point or center of attention. You might feel fearful and/or nervous about introducing yourself or running into someone from your past. You might feel terrified around authority figures. You might even have trouble ordering food at a restaurant. Or you might have a problem being assertive and standing up for yourself. Basically, any scene, situation, or small interaction that necessitates your dealing with another person or other people is fair game for this list.

2. Give each situation a SUDS level from zero to one hundred. The SUDS scale was invented by South African psychiatrist Joseph Wolpe in 1969. The acronym stands for "Subjective Units of Distress." It provides an individual a way to measure how intense their emotions feel in a given situation, and to compare them with other situations.

Wolpe's original SUDS model listed degrees of anxiety from one to ten (completely relaxed to total nervous breakdown). I suggest being even more granular and using a scale from zero to one hundred. The levels break down like this:

- *Zero to twenty-four: No distress.* You're pretty much free and relaxed in this situation, with only moderate flutters, if any. This could mean lying in bed reading a book, taking a long bath, knitting—casual leisure time, basically.

- *Twenty-five to forty-nine: Mild anxiety.* You're in a situation that causes you to feel a little uneasy or cautiously aware, but you're not entirely terrified and you're still in control. This level of anxiety can be associated with moments of preparation: a bar patron getting their nerve up to sing at karaoke night, somebody waiting for their blind date to show up at a restaurant, and so forth. You're not in the thick of it and you're still safe, but you're mildly concerned about what's coming.

- *Fifty to sixty-four: Moderate distress.* You're starting to feel around the edges of panic here. You're not in meltdown mode—you're still fully able to handle the situation—but you're slightly preoccupied with your fears and might be figuring out ways to avoid them. You could be avoiding eye contact with others or sitting still. You're starting to feel discomfort and having some unpleasant thoughts. Examples include having a mild but not heated disagreement with a friend, or being in a bar where the customers are very, very different from you.

- *Sixty-five to eighty-four: On high alert.* At this stage, you're starting to freak out. You're finding it hard to handle a situation. You're having a hard time focusing on what's going on. You might be in the early stages of planning an escape route. You're able to stay in control, but not easily. You can see the meltdown coming, but you're not in mortal danger. This could be when the argument with your friend turns nasty or insulting, or if you're on a crowded subway car feeling threatened and claustrophobic.

- *Eighty-five to one hundred: Mortal danger.* Okay, *now* you're freaking out. The fallout is happening, and it's severe. Your body is reacting in extreme discomfort. You feel you need to escape but can't see how. You're scared about what you might possibly do and you're out of control of your emotions. You're paralyzed and in a physical and mental panic. You may not be able to function at all. The nervous breakdown is either just around the corner or staring you in the face. Welcome to Defcon 1.

Going back to your list of apprehensive situations, give each one of them a SUDS rating. Make sure you're grading each according to how well or badly you *feel*, as opposed to how bad you think you *appear*. This should be based on your internal reactions only.

For example, say you don't particularly enjoy parties. You feel self-conscious and awkward. You might be at a party where you don't know anyone when you get there, and it makes you a little uneasy. You might rate that situation something around fifty-five or sixty. But when someone you know and trust shows up and you can spend a little time talking to them at the party, the rating might go down to twenty-five or lower. Or maybe nobody you know shows up and other party guests start looking at you in a strange way that you perceive as being threatening. In that situation, the anxiety level might be closer to eighty. It probably won't get higher unless a massive brawl breaks out.

By now, you should have a pretty comprehensive list of anxious situations and their relative level of distress. Now it's time to figure out which of them you'd like to tackle first. Remember: we're talking about a very gradual, step-by-step program here. The situations you address first should be meaningful, but at this stage, your goals for growth and change need to be realistic.

3. Plan your goals. Should you be assigning SUDS levels to anything that crosses your mind? No, be specific in what you want to achieve. Select the situations you want to fix the most. Start with the ones that are most important to you. Ideally your first batch of goals should cover a wide range of SUDS levels, from easy to hard. For a handy way to decide which goals are appropriate for this stage, you might want to measure them against a set of criteria expressed in the acronym "PRAMS":

- *Personal.* Select situations that mean the most to you at present. They might be situations you face every day, or ones that affect a bunch of different areas of your life. For example, you might want to combat your social fears of work-related events, because not attending might adversely affect your relationship with co-workers.

- *Realistic.* Pick specific goals that are within the realm of possibility. You can't expect that you can completely rid yourself of worry or become a social butterfly overnight. Go with the goals that are within the scope of gradual change. Instead of choosing the goal, "I want to feel one hundred percent at ease with my entire family," make the goal something like, "I want to have a weekly lunch with my sister."

- *Achievable.* Choose goals that are within your reach right now. You may have a greater vision in mind, but pick a goal that you can accomplish given whatever resources and time you have at present. For example, it might be too much to expect that you'll immediately be able to address a crowd of five hundred people—but maybe ten people is entirely possible. You don't have to feel like it's achievable tomorrow, simply achievable within a reasonable time frame.

- *Measurable.* As much as possible, go for goals for which it's easy to track your progress. Don't opt for general goals with vague ambitions—instead of "I want to feel completely comfortable talking in a bar," try, "I want to hold my own in conversation at a bar for fifteen minutes."

- *Specific.* Get as exact and precise as possible. You're taking baby steps in this exercise. For example, if one of the situations you avoid is going to parties, your goal might be, "Attend my cousin's baby shower at the end of this month." That's all you need to do right now. Later on, you can shoot for the opening-night gala.

4. Build your goal stepladder. You've planned a goal and have decided to start work. Remember, situational exposure is a bit-by-bit process. Even though your goal might (and should) be a specific one, it's best to approach it as a large task comprised of several smaller tasks. This is by far the most important aspect of exposure therapy and taking action toward gaining confidence. Without a clear goal stepladder or sequence of events, you'll never get started because it will never stop feeling too scary. Remember, if the goal is to gradually gain control over a fear, you need to be strategic about the tasks.

The top of the stepladder represents your ultimate goal in this task, and the steps represent each smaller task that eventually gets you to the top. The bottom step is the goal that you tackle first, one that you can achieve without an intense amount of anxiety. Each progressive step builds in intensity as you climb toward your goal.

For example, say one of your goals is to improve your confidence at an important work-related social function taking place in three weeks. Currently, you can't handle more than ten minutes without shaking or stammering. You usually try to find excuses not to go. You'd like to change that, and you've decided to take it on in smaller chunks.

You've figured that it would probably be sufficient if you could stay at this work function and mingle for two hours. That is the top of your stepladder — along with your SUDS estimation of how anxious you'd feel if you had to do that right now:

Mingle at company function for two hours: seventy-eight.

You have three weeks to accomplish this. Sounds like plenty of time. But you have to lead up to it with a set of subtasks that gradually increase with intensity. Starting with the first step, pick a smaller goal that's relatively easy to execute right now—and don't be ashamed if it's so easy it's ridiculous:

Have a coffee break with a close friend who knows you well for fifteen minutes: thirty-one. In this particular step, the "close friend" should be someone who knows about the issues you're having. That's the easiest place to start, and you're sure you'll feel more comfortable than anxious. Then, pick the next step:

Have lunch with your close friend for thirty minutes: thirty-eight. The only things that are changing in this step are how much time you're allotting and probably what you're eating. That's how incremental this can be. Now we pick up the pace:

Have an after-work coffee or drink with your close friend for thirty minutes: forty-two. Assuming you work nine to five (adjust as needed), the first two steps probably took place in a familiar environment. Now that it's after work, the venue will probably change to a place you're not one hundred percent comfy with. But you still have your friend with you. Then:

Have an after-work coffee or drink with your close friend and two other people you know well for forty-five minutes: forty-eight. Your social fears happen to be tied to people you don't know intimately, or casual acquaintances. There's a little bit more at risk in this situation. But it's still accomplishable—you're already at the fourth step. Here's the fifth:

Have a group lunch at work with three other members of your department you know, but not intimately, for sixty minutes: fifty-four. Your close friend isn't your safety net anymore. But you're with people you probably see every single day, so there's at least a bit of familiarity. And this could be a preface to getting to know them better. Then:

Have an after-work drink in a bar with three members of your department, and a trusted supervisor if you can swing it, for sixty minutes: sixty-three. You're outside your familiar terrain. You're in an unmonitored situation. And if you can handle it (it's okay if you can't), you're with a person with some authority or managerial sway over you. You're so close. Then:

Have an after-work drink in a bar with five members of your department, some of *their* guests, and a trusted supervisor if you can

swing it, for two hours: sixty-nine. More people, more time, more progress. Then, finally:

Mingle at a company function for two hours: seventy-eight. You're at the top of your stepladder. How's the view?

Your actual stepladder might contain fewer or more steps than this one, and that's fine. And depending on how your low self-esteem or lack of confidence manifests, you may choose completely different steps or ways of achieving each step.

What's important is that you only need to do what you're capable of at any given step. There's nothing wrong with admitting you need to add more steps in. In other words, if the steps are too big, break them down further. Just keep going. And of course, expect that overall goals with higher SUDS ratings will probably need to have more steps than those that stir up less anxiety. Just take each goal and step into careful and honest self-consideration.

Even though exposure therapy works, sometimes we need to take a step back to make it feel easier. Some people may need to start from a place you might consider to have extremely low SUDS levels, and that's okay. Exposure therapy is a rather big commitment, and there are ways to engage in action outside of it.

For instance, as a preliminary step, you can commit to smiling at a stranger once a day—SUDS level: seven. That's all it takes to begin. In most cases, they will repay your smile with a smile of their own. Now, that wasn't so horrible, was it?

Once you have accomplished this small step, you can move on to saying hello or waving to people as a form of social pleasantry—SUDS level: fifteen. You can build on this by doing all the above and then asking people a question in addition—SUDS level: twenty-two. One day, you can wear mismatched socks to see if anyone comments—SUDS level: eight. You can also ask people for the time of day—SUDS level: fourteen. Ask someone to take a picture of you—SUDS level: twenty. Start from a point that creates so little stress that it barely feels like you are doing anything.

There are additional steps you can take that allow you to experience a degree of fear and uncertainty, but in safe situations and thereby similarly keeping the SUDS levels relatively low. In a sense, these are all ways to practice exposure with a safety net.

Situation #1: Doing the action you fear, but in an easier or less intense setting.

Suppose that you experience anxiety about speaking to new people. If that's the case, you'll want to try speaking with someone you don't know, but in an easy, safe, and non-threatening circumstance.

A good example of this would be chatting up the barista at your favorite coffee bar, or the cashier at the market, or any service personnel that is attending to you. They are accustomed to making small talk with customers, so they will help make it easy for you—and the encounter carries no risk because nothing is at stake. Even better, it will be short. It will only last as long as your credit card takes to swipe, and that's a relief for most.

Speak to a barista or cashier for one or two more sentences than you normally would. Ask how they are and what they are doing this weekend. Ask if the store has been busy. Ask if they have had the food or coffee that you are ordering and what they think about it.

Ask a stranger for the time or easy directions. Ask someone to take a picture of you in front of a building. Do this once every other day, and you'll be off to a great start. You're still doing the same basic action you fear, but you are choosing your battles wisely to increase the chances that you'll walk away with a more positive outcome and a successful notch in your belt.

Situation #2: Do something similar to the situation you fear that brings up the same feelings.

Let's take the same example and say your anxiety is speaking to strangers.

What happens to you in this situation? You might feel anxious, stressed, your palms sweat, and you stumble over your words. What situations are similar to having to speak to strangers?

Some examples could be opening a door for someone, riding in an elevator with someone, having to call a customer service number to ask a question, playing a team sport, or even chatting in an anonymous internet chat room. Whatever the case, allow yourself to engage in different social interactions while feeling the same tension as your desired goal.

Situation #3: Practice the exact thing you fear, but in a controlled setting.

Luckily, there are numerous groups, both social and professional (and clinical!) that exist for this very purpose. After all, people are typically willing to help you by conducting practice interviews, and this is not too different. The first controlled setting you can use is simply to role play a conversation with a friend.

Toastmasters is another example of a controlled setting. Toastmasters is a public speaking group where members engage in planned or impromptu speeches, each meant to help the speaker become more comfortable with public speaking and destroy their fears.

Finally, you can even engage in role playing or exercise with a trained professional. A therapist can walk you through situations and build your confidence and skills because that is their very purpose. Again, the important part is that you are in a safe setting. Nobody is going to judge you. Nobody is going to make you feel uncomfortable and awkward.

You know that these situations are controlled and there will be no unpredictable surprises. Their SUDS levels are low. They can be steppingstones to work up to the process of exposure therapy, or they might even be enough on their own. What's certain is that starting small, so it barely feels like you are even taking action, can help you sidestep fear and claim the confidence you are seeking.

By the way, you could choose to forego entirely the incremental steps. This would be through something known as *radical implosion*, which is something psychologist Albert Ellis coined. This is the proverbial version of jumping immediately into the deep end and forcing yourself to swim. He describes his introduction to the concept in 1933, when he attempted to approach every woman who sat alone in a garden: "Thirty walked away immediately," he told the *New York Times*. "I talked with the other hundred for the first time in my life, no matter how anxious I was. Nobody vomited and ran away. Nobody called the cops."

It's not for the faint of heart, but certainly represents an alternative to slowly building up your confidence through small steps.

You might be wondering how this applies to you if your low confidence doesn't manifest primarily in social settings. The principle, however, is the same. Anxiety and low self-esteem are so intimately connected that for many people, they are more or less the same thing. But if you're the kind of person who feels able to function socially while still feeling unconfident, then it doesn't mean you can't use exposure therapy, only that the things you expose yourself to will be different.

For example, you might devise a way to work up to asking someone for help, opening up to them emotionally, revealing something a little intimate about yourself, or having the confidence to set and assert a healthy boundary. For you, confidence may look like living more genuinely and sharing your true opinions more freely, or it may mean having the guts to finally take the chance at a big dream you've left unfulfilled.

The Alter Ego

A final note on how to make action easier is the concept of the *alter ego*. Have you ever put on a mask for Halloween? Everyone you came in contact with that day knew you were wearing a mask. They might have even known it was you behind it. But admit it: wasn't it just the least bit *empowering*?

You might have felt, however rightly or not, that you couldn't be held responsible for what you did or said, because you could just blame it on the role later. "That wasn't me! That was Captain Jack Sparrow!" "I didn't eat all the snacks—that was Fat Albert! He eats everything!"

Of course, those excuses don't hold up after the fact. But when you're playing a role, especially if you have the costume to go with it, you probably take on a little bit of your character's traits and mannerisms. And it probably comes very easily.

One of the best ways to act (when acting is out of character) is by creating an alter ego because of the surprising feeling of power and control it can give you. During Halloween, you might feel emboldened and empowered—imagine how great it would be to apply that sort of feeling to everyday situations. This is how you can truly get through exposure therapy and the like, even if you are frightened as can be.

For our purposes, an alter ego is a second self created by an individual, usually for the purposes to live out a "better" version of the self.

In comic books, Bruce Wayne runs his multimillion-dollar business every day. Peter Parker works as a photographer for the *Daily Bugle*. But when a crisis hits the cities they live in and the usual authority figures are unable to handle it, they morph into their crime-fighting alter egos, Batman and Spiderman. The city is saved, usually with a little property damage, but still saved.

Pop music artists are frequent adopters of the alter ego. When they take the stage, they have to push out a larger-than-life spectacle that takes more than their everyday, regular selves to pull off. All pop musicians do that to some extent, but some go even further by creating elaborate personas.

For a time, the great British performer David Bowie changed personas seemingly at will. The best-known was Ziggy Stardust, a humanoid alien who's something of an extraterrestrial messenger. Ziggy let Bowie distance himself from the boy from Beckenham and take on a fearless, heroic personality.

In 2008, American singer and songwriter Beyoncé Knowles created her own alter ego, Sasha Fierce. This character was fun, sensual, glamorous, and aggressive—all of which were on full display in her video "Single Ladies." Apart from her Sasha persona, Beyoncé was reserved, polite, and genial. But her alter ego was the vehicle for singing and saying things that might not have been as effectively conveyed using her everyday image.

An alter ego encompasses the best parts of what you want to be and gives you full license to do what you couldn't do as yourself. At the very least, it allows you to ask what someone else would do and witness the separation between your answer to the same question.

An alter ego that's well thought out can help you bridge the gap between where you are now and where you want to be. It lets you step out of the box you've created for yourself in public and do something that's totally out of character. The imaginative process you take in creating and being that alter ego might provide clues on how to make those improvements in your real life. Finally, it just lets you ask, "What would my fearless alter ego do?" which is a more productive question to answer than, "What should I do here if I know I should be brave but am still scared?"

Having an alter ego, as we've mentioned, is empowering. After switching characters, you have a window of opportunity when you can be brave and detach yourself from your hang-ups. That window of time is when you push against your comfort zone and try new things.

Like Bowie did with Ziggy, you can channel your confidence through your alter ego. Sure, Bowie could have sung all the Ziggy songs dressed in a T-shirt and jeans while not wearing any makeup. But by taking on another character, Bowie turned those songs into a whole new drama with graspable themes, storylines, and excitement. It was a gambit that let him display his creativity to its fullest.

Every time you're about to try a new endeavor, there's a little voice in your head that begins whining and advising you. This is your actual ego, the one Freud described. Its job, as we discussed earlier, is to be the reasonable one in any new situation.

And when faced with a new situation, your ego gets a little jittery: "What are you doing? Stop! What if you look stupid? What will everyone think? What if they all laugh at you? Who do you think you are, anyway—you're not brave or smart or strong enough to do this! Let's just go home and watch *The Little Mermaid* again!"

That's when an alter ego comes to the rescue, bolts past your ego's whimpering, and leads you out of the comfort zone. Where the ego expresses fear, the alter-ego is rarin' to go. "Hey! This looks great! This looks exciting! Let's get started now!"

The ego then says, "But what will everybody say? You're just setting this person up for ridicule!" To which the alter ego responds, "Oh, forget them. If they don't have anything better to do than gossip, let 'em talk. They can think whatever they want. It's not going to get in our way. I got no use for 'em."

Finally, the ego cries, "But what if I *fail*?" And the alter ego says, "If you try it, yeah, you might fail—but you might *succeed*. Whereas, if you *don't* try, you'll *definitely* fail. Excuse me, I'm running late."

Let's say you're starting a new job, for which you feel grateful but a little under qualified. Your ego is shaking in its boots— "I'm not ready for this! I can't do all the things they'll expect me to do!"

Your alter ego: "Fantastic! I can't wait to jump in! I'm going to take charge of this sucker—I'll be too busy to be bored!"

Ego: "But they'll be disappointed! They were expecting someone else with more experience and knowledge than I have!"

Alter Ego: "You bet they are—they're expecting *me*! And boy oh boy, are they gonna get me!"

Ego: "If I don't work out, they're going to fire me and I'm going to be destitute and broke! I can't do this!"

Alter Ego: "Oh, no they won't. I'm far too powerful for them. I can do anything. I can do several things at once. I can do *their* jobs as well! In fact, just for fun, I think I'm going to do just that! This is a funhouse of opportunity, and I'm knockin' on that door, baby!"

Your results—and inner dialogue—may vary. Not only are you speaking in the terms of your alter ego, but you're also treating your *comfort zone's* ego as an objective, other character as well. You can verbalize what it is about that comfort zone that you want to change and let your alter ego run with it.

So you've decided you're going to don the cap or put on the breastplate—metaphorically speaking, probably—and indulge yourself in the character of an alter ego. How do you go about it?

Determine why you want an alter ego. Ask yourself what's spurring you to develop an alter ego and what you hope to achieve. Do you want to be more outgoing, confident, or unique? Do you need someone to stand up for you? Do you just want more people to read your blog or watch your YouTube videos? In what way will they be assisting in breaking you out of your comfort zone?

Your alter ego should have some sort of purpose or mission. Remember, you're looking for empowerment, an avenue by which you can express yourself in a new context. You're putting your hopes, dreams, fears, and insecurities into this alter ego, giving them the kind of abilities that you don't have as a mortal human. Your alter ego doesn't necessarily have to live by the rules, but it should have a *point.*

Develop your alter ego's personality. What type of person does your alter ego have to be to achieve the goals you're after? How do they think? What's their mindset? What models are you using to build their thoughts or actions?

You have an unlimited range of options to choose from. You could just use the alter ego as a reflection or extrapolation of yourself to imbue a personality that you'd like to someday inhabit. Conversely, you can make it your polar opposite to investigate a total contrast of yourself to help you understand the "other side." The answers you're looking for are largely going to come from the type of attitudes and voicing your alter ego has, so develop them as fully as you can.

Make sure you can describe your alter ego, without hesitation, using five positive adjectives. These are the traits you are striving toward.

Flesh out the details. The secondary part of your alter ego's story will be how they'd present themselves to the rest of the world—so give them a name and an appearance. Again, you have no restrictions here. You might be a T-shirt and jeans person, but your alter ego could be a high-fashion hound with garish fur coats and sparkling sunglasses. Or perhaps they'll only wear black and disappear underneath the hood of their sweatshirt.

Spend time developing your alter ego's mannerisms. How do they walk? What does their voice sound like? How do they wear their hair, or do they wear hats? Do they speak the King's English or do they have some kind of accent? The more details you can provide for your alter ego, the easier it will be to slip into their character.

Try to come up with a significant and meaningful name. You can base it on someone you admire, the name of your superhero, a take on another fictional character, or one from history. You could just attach a superlative to the end of your name— "Felix the Great"—or spell your name backward. Have some sort of justification or explanation for the name, even if it's random. As with appearances, the more detail you can invent, the more tangible the alter ego will feel.

Activate! An alter ego should respond to some kind of call to action, something to invoke them when they're needed. Captain Marvel called out to his gods, who then graciously struck him with lightning and turned him into a superhero. Batman was channeled into action by an extremely powerful, custom-made flashlight that seemingly every household in Gotham had. The alter-ego rock band KISS took to the stage with the announcer's cry, "You wanted the best . . . you *got* the best! The hottest band in the world, KISS!"

You could come up with a rallying cry, something that could theoretically fit on a T-shirt or hat. You could cue up a song that would announce the alter ego's arrival, or something that would just pump you up. You could throw red roses in its pathway, unfurl a flag or carpet, clang on a cowbell—whatever works.

The activation routine is important because it's meant to snap you out of your mood and take on the alter ego's spirit. If you feel sad, it's extraordinarily difficult to just "decide" you feel happy. Some sort of catalyst, calling, or benediction can help turn that alternate mood on.

Remember, this isn't just escapism. A lot of people do role-play or cosplay for recreational reasons. While you should have fun with your alter ego, you're not just creating it to escape into a fantasy world. You invented it to figure out a solution of some sort to achieve a certain goal.

Ask yourself how your alter ego would act in the process of accomplishing your purpose. Give this a lot of conscious thought. Then act that way. Create a distance from your own self, and "storyboard" how your creation would perform in the situation at hand. How would James Bond deal with your overbearing boss? How would Gollum from *Lord of the Rings* make a marriage proposal? How would Darth Vader handle himself at your in-laws' Thanksgiving dinner?

You know how *you'll* act. That's why creating a distance from that is important. Your alter ego encourages you to act quicker, sharper, and braver because you're taking yourself out of the picture. You're not thinking about yourself anymore. You're thinking about a woodland nymph, an astronaut, Marilyn Monroe, and the Incredible Hulk.

Identity diversification

Speaking of alter egos, let's take a closer look— what is it about having a "mask" that helps you feel more confident in yourself? Picture this. A person is a workaholic who derives their *entire* sense of identity from their ability to do this one thing perfectly. What happens when they don't do that thing well one day? Their entire sense of self-worth evaporates.

Identity diversification turns this on its head— basically, the more sources of good feelings and confidence you have, the more robust your identity, and the harder it is to knock you off kilter. If you derive good feelings from being good at your job, a good spouse, a talented artist, *and* a fabulous parent, then messing up in one area doesn't feel like such a disaster. It's like making sure you're not putting all your confidence eggs in one basket.

In the same way as you diversify an investment portfolio, you can spread the risk of damage to your self-identity by working on many different aspects of yourself, and not just one. Even if you encounter a psychological setback or upset, you are still shored up elsewhere. Life is complex and unpredictable. But if you "diversify your identity," you multiply the sources of good feelings while moderating any potential problems in any one area.

So, ask yourself—where does your validation, self-esteem, identity, and contentment come from?

What do you identify with and where do you place your identity?

Yes, we know it's good to derive a sense of worth *internally*, but even still, do we have a multifaceted and robust sense of this picture of ourselves?

For example, person A has unconsciously made their romantic relationship the be-all-and-end-all of their life. When their relationship is going well, everything is right with the world, but when it isn't, there's nothing else to fall back on, and it all collapses. Person B might derive a lot of satisfaction and meaning from their relationship, but they don't focus on it alone— instead, they have many different answers to the question, "What makes you who you are?"

They take pride in their physical fitness, they work hard, they identify as being intelligent or creative or a good communicator (or whatever the case may be), and they have a strong sense of identity in their family or groups they belong to.

People with one singular focus in life might make for good celebrities or characters in dramatic plays, but they are seldom balanced and resilient human beings:

- The mom who doesn't even know who she is anymore once her kids grow up and fly the nest

- The overachieving student who is lost once they graduate and leave academia

- The beautiful woman who painfully discovers at forty years of age that she has never really developed any other aspect of her identity than her appearance

- The man who identifies strongly with his social class and his wealth, who feels suicidal and worthless when he is suddenly bankrupted and broke

- The person who is so wrapped up in their vision of themselves as a winner, that when they lose, they find it almost unbearable

In the context of confidence, we can see that not only is it risky to invest your sense of worth and identity in external things, but it's especially risky to invest it in just one thing. Granted, the examples above show just how culturally defined these patterns are— "perfection" for women stereotypically means beauty, for men it means wealth, for students it means never losing, for parents it means complete and utter devotion, and so on.

Many of us are steeped in social worlds that overvalue celebrity, or "hustle culture," or images of perfection and high achievement. We are told to aim high and never give up until we get there. Be single-minded, work hard, and you'll excel eventually. The entrepreneurs, artists, and athletes are held up as models of the highest human achievement.

But really, how many of our culture's heroes are the kind of people who we'd consider obsessive or unhealthy if we met them in a more everyday context? While they focused single-mindedly on just one project, every other area of their life may have suffered. Many glittering tech billionaires are awful partners and parents, have few genuine friendships, neglect their physical health, and have nothing to show in the way of spiritual, cultural, or artistic development.

And what about those people who followed this superstar path but *weren't* so successful? In other words, there are people out there who diligently followed the ultra-obsessed and singular path trodden by the likes of Steve Jobs or Oprah or Michael Jordan, but for whatever reason failed in their attempt. You'll recognize the underlying all-or-nothing logic as a kind of fallacious way of thinking: either you are the ultimate, high-achieving superhero of your wildest dreams—or you're nothing. And the world is filled with very few Steve Jobs and Oprah Winfrey types, and far, far higher numbers of people who tried to succeed in just one area and failed.

Tying yourself in any way to just one person, one role, one experience, one belief, or one perspective is by definition limiting. You are ensuring that you are less flexible, and you shut yourself out from other sources of meaning, contentment, purpose, value. You may pass over opportunities to learn something new or discover that your current beliefs aren't as good as you thought they were. In fact, after a while, the sheer fact of you being so narrowly focused becomes a reason to keep on stubbornly with the same project. You become the person who thinks, "Maybe this new thing is better, but I don't care. I've been doing this old thing for ages and it's too late to stop now, and besides, I'm comfortable and I don't want to face the idea that I might have been wrong all this time."

Those who limit themselves to just one path (no matter how glamorous or noble that one path) are choosing a two-dimensional, monotonous existence that lacks the potential for growth. When we overidentify with one aspect of life at the expense of the others, we open ourselves up to risk. But if our sense of identity and worth is evenly distributed over a range of (changing) aspects and ideas, then we tolerate uncertainty and challenge better, we adapt and learn, and we can do the difficulty work of letting go of what truly isn't working for us anymore.

The irony is that it's hating the feeling of uncertainty that drives us to cling to one particular source of identity, but in doing so, we are actually more at risk for having our confidence smashed when things in that area don't go to plan. Seeking familiarity, stability, and certainty are, ironically, the things that will guarantee we will be unprepared for change or difficulty when it arises. In this state of mind, our world shrinks, and with it, our adaptability and resilience.

You might not even be sure of exactly where you have been investing your identity until that source is seriously threatened. You'll know that you've overinvested if a small setback in one area seems to threaten your entire sense of self-worth and belief in who you are. This is a strong signal that it's time to have other things in your life. No, your identity doesn't have to be a chaotic, super-complex mix of many different interests, skills, and beliefs. It just needs to be rounded and versatile. It needs to help you face a disaster with the confidence to say, "That's okay, I can survive that. This one single thing is not all I am."

How to Achieve More Identity Diversification

Try an exercise to visualize exactly where you have invested your own feelings of confidence. With a pen and paper, jot down a few answers to the question, **"What makes me who I am?"**

Imagine that feelings of confidence, competence, and self-worth are flowing in—where do they come from? Maybe the roles you play (parent, spouse, employee, teacher), the groups you belong to, the actions you perform, or the traits you possess. If you like, rate each with a number on a scale of one to ten, or visualize it as proportions of a pie chart. Is a huge chunk of your confidence coming from just a single place? Time to make a change.

Pick three *other* areas that you already derive some validation, pride, meaning, or contentment from. For each one, choose an action you can take *today* that will more firmly cement this in your life. For example, you might decide to enroll in a course to better learn a skill, invest in an interesting book, or start a project that develops your interest or capabilities in this area. Repeat the exercise in six months' time to see if you feel more balanced and rounded. For example, instead of your identity being, "I'm a lawyer," you can now confidently say, "I'm a lawyer, mother, and ceramics artist who loves horse-riding and reading experimental poetry."

Mindfulness to Reduce Anxiety and Overthinking

Our final consideration for this chapter is an idea that has more or less been implied throughout—that mindful awareness is the first step toward better confidence. This is because by practicing mindful presence in the moment, we can become aware of the negative thought patterns controlling our lives and make conscious, informed decisions to do something different.

But mindfulness has another powerful benefit, and that's to lower anxiety. When we are relaxed and calm, we are no longer being driven by fear or triggered into anxious overthinking. It's a "virtuous cycle": the more serenity we have, the easier it is to look at things with clarity and balance, and the more we do this, the more we can remove sources of anxiety from our lives in the first place.

Is mindfulness and meditation a way of life, a special practice, or a therapeutic technique to help with some particular problem? Actually, it can be all three.
We can try to cultivate a general sense of mindfulness as we go about our daily lives, but we can also dedicate some time to practicing a more formal sitting meditation routine. Finally, we can use the principles of mindfulness in a more acute way, as a stress-management technique.

Mindfulness can be a real solution to a hyper-stressful society. Mindfulness-based stress reduction is now studied in universities all over the world as a practical method for stress management. Furthermore, by using any of the approaches outlined in previous chapters, you give yourself the chance to avoid activating the stress response in the first place.

Mindfulness can teach you to take your thoughts a little less seriously, and switch from a hectic "doing" mode to a simpler "being" mode. By reining in your reactivity, you create space to respond more moderately, taking into account how your body feels rather than remaining entirely in your head. With compassion and acceptance, your entire attitude toward stress and adversity changes— you are less likely to respond with judgment and panic and more likely to be compassionate with yourself and others, and find calm, focused solutions to problems.

Many of us can diligently stick to a meditation practice when times are okay, but find it enormously challenging to remain consciously aware during times of crisis. Luckily, you can use meditation as a more deliberate response to stressful situations.

Start as you would any other meditation session, i.e. get comfortable, find your breath and posture, and get into a calm and relaxed state of mind.

Take your time to flesh this stressful situation out in your mind's eye. Imagine it vividly, immersing yourself in the picture. Notice where the stress expresses itself on your body—do you feel tight across your shoulders, or tension in your jawline? Breathe into this and stay with it for a moment.

Next, notice your emotional state. Use kind and

accepting attention to really inhabit your feelings. You may even place a hand on the location on your body where you feel pain or discomfort, as though you were comforting a friend or a scared child.

Remember that you are not there to fix anything. You are not trying to soothe out a rough patch, or convince yourself not to feel how you feel, or draw a curtain over the experience and forget about it. All you are doing is being with the stressful sensation, without judgment, without looking to the next moment, without looking for ways to deny or avoid.

This technique may seem counterintuitive to those who are chronically stressed—doesn't sitting with stress simply make you more anxious?

The trick is that you are not ruminating any further or engaging in any planning, strategizing, interpreting, judging, solving, or appraising. You are just there to *be*. There's no need to devise a story about what you're experiencing and why, or to push or pull against it. You are not explicitly trying to calm yourself down, but feeling calmer is a typical side effect of this practice. What you are primarily doing is **meeting your stressful experience head-on, in the moment, with**

nothing but kind attention.

Nevertheless, there are countless relaxation techniques that can be used to actively soothe and calm a stressed-out mind, and these can be employed in conjunction with a mindfulness-based practice. Deep breathing is one such technique that can powerfully release stress in the body, and can be combined with almost every other stress-management activity.

One breathing technique is called square breathing. Lie on the floor with one hand on your chest and one on your belly. Breathe in through your nose and into your stomach, feeling it rise as you count slowly from one to four. Try to move the hand on your chest as little as possible, while breathing deeply and fully into your belly. Hold the breath for another four counts, then breathe out. As you breathe out, ease the air slowly out through your mouth for another four counts. You may purse your lips to help slow down your exhalation.

Not only does belly breathing fill your body with oxygen, slow your heart rate, and decrease your blood pressure, it also stimulates the vagus nerve, which instigates a relaxation response across your entire body and makes you feel calmer.

Deep-breathing exercises work to ease tension and chaos in your mind as the slow, steady breaths are incompatible with the quick, shallow breaths typical of the stress response. So instead of your mental and emotional state dictating how your body reacts, you can reverse the process and have your body—through slow, deep breaths—influence your mind to be serene and composed.

A "body scan" is another wonderful stress management and relaxation technique that can be used with or without meditation and mindfulness. Again, the body is an anchor into the present moment, and a point of focus to bring back a wandering mind.

Lie down somewhere comfortable where you won't be disturbed for a while, uncross your arms and legs, and close your eyes. Take a few moments to slow down and focus on your breath for a moment. Then, as though your consciousness were like a spotlight, shine your awareness on different parts of your body one at a time.

Start at your feet. Focus on nothing but the sensation of having your feet—what can you feel?

With awareness, you might notice you can actually sense the skin across the surface of your foot, the weight of your heel pressing into the floor, or the soft fabric of your socks against your toes. You can focus on each toe individually, starting from one side and moving through all ten toes, spending a good few seconds on each one, just checking in with it and observing how it feels.

As you notice sensations, let go of any judgments about what is good or bad, or what certain sensations mean. If you find you are tense somewhere, you don't need to immediately jump in and relax those muscles—just become aware. After a moment, you might like to breathe more deeply into the feeling, whatever it is, and notice if more relaxation arises.

Then move on to the soles of your feet and then heels, lavishing complete attention on each part without rushing. Move on to your ankles, then slowly up your body, to your calves, knees, thighs, hips, belly, and so on until you are focusing on your chin, eyes, forehead, even your scalp. Of course, the body is all one piece, so it's up to you which parts you decide to zero in on and how long you linger.

If you encounter pain, discomfort, an itch, or a strange sensation, linger a little longer there. Breathe deeply and imagine the breath flowing through your body, moving to the area, bringing space and awareness so it can just be what it is. Notice any areas where you feel extra sensitive and inflamed, as well as places you feel numb. In scanning your body, you are simply trying to see where and how you are. Fully inhabit the sensations you encounter without pushing against them.

A body scan is an excellent way to start or end a more formal meditative practice, and is also a great standalone relaxation technique at bedtime or during stressful periods. It's a technique that can encourage body-mind connection and can alert you to the tiny physiological events and sensations that would otherwise be missed by a busy mind.

Some people like to combine a body scan with elements of visualization—i.e. the practice of using your mind's eye to imagine a scene or imagery, usually for relaxation purposes. In traditional meditation, images are not deliberately conjured up; rather, the mind's activities are observed without attachment. But with visualization, you deliberately give your mind a soothing image or scene to focus on.

Essentially, you begin as you would any other meditation practice—sit or lie quietly somewhere and focus for a moment on the breath. Eyes closed, try to conjure up an image of something restful or calming, like a serene beach, a beautiful fantasy landscape, a cozy room with gentle rain outside and crackling fire in the corner, or an ancient temple strewn with petals.

Take your time to really flesh out this place— the sights, sounds, smells, tastes, and even feelings it evokes. Imagine even the tiniest details and textures. You may find it easier at first to do a guided meditation where the scene is described to you and you are prompted to explore it, or you can make your own recording to personalize your guided visualization. You may like to add appropriate white noise or nature sounds to complete the experience, although this isn't necessary.

Engage all your senses and let your busy mind still for a moment. Forget about worries and rumination. In your visualization, you can do what you want—picture a ball of radiant gold light that you step into to feel safe and happy, or bathe in a magical fountain that washes away stress. Imagine yourself standing in a hazy glade of enormous trees, grass between your toes, as the wind blows over every part of you, taking your anxieties away with it. It's up to you!

If these relaxation techniques sound a little too time-consuming, don't worry, they needn't be. You can experience effective stress relief and relaxation in just a few minutes. Try a quick three-minute breathing practice: begin in the first minute by asking, "How am I right now?" Spend a minute checking in with your thoughts and feelings, and put a name to the sensations or emotions you're experiencing.

In the next minute, sink deeper into simply being aware of your breath. If thoughts and feelings emerge, gently let them go and return to the breath, in and out. For the final minute, go into your body—spread awareness out over your physical experience in the moment.

This may seem like a simple and straightforward practice, but it very quickly teaches you to pause, become aware of your mental and emotional state, and then ground down into the present reality, as it's felt in your breath and your body. Within three minutes, you can quickly reorient yourself, let go of stress, and give yourself a window in the day to really remember who you are and what you're doing.

Finally, no discussion of relaxation techniques is complete without considering stretching. Bearing in mind what we know about making certain behaviors automatic habits, consider adding on a relaxing stretching practice to the beginning or end of your normal exercise routine. Not only will you avoid rushing into physical activity and risking injury, but you'll give yourself a chance to really check in, be present, and notice how you're actually doing in the moment.

Stretching improves flexibility and boosts circulation—not to mention it just feels good! Although yoga certainly has benefits, you don't have to do a full yoga practice. Stretching is an intuitive human activity we all know how to do. Nevertheless, take care not to stretch to the point of pain, and go slowly and gently.

Try this: take a few deep breaths before you start, then move into the stretch until you feel that familiar pull—not pain. Now, still in position, relax the muscle as much as possible. Then, tighten or tense it again, still in position, before fully relaxing it once more. From here, you can stretch a little further than your previous limit. You can repeat the process as often as you like, but make sure you're going slowly and breathing deeply throughout.

When you stretch, stay mindful and be present with how it feels. Notice any asymmetries in your body, tight or sore spots, or places where you can feel the effects of a workout. It makes a lot of sense to combine stretching, relaxation techniques, meditation, and daily exercise. You can establish a daily flow and routine that gets you moving but also more relaxed and mindful, ready to return to the rest of your day feeling refreshed and calm.

Takeaways:

- Sometimes, talk is cheap. At the very least, talking your way to confidence through recognizing cognitive distortions and engaging in cognitive behavioral therapy is a slow and unwieldy process. Action, on the other hand, gets things done a little bit quicker.

- When we think about confidence, we want to feel confident and comfortable before taking action. But that's the wrong way of looking at it and will leave you waiting and searching far longer than you should. Instead, you should understand that action *causes* confidence. The power of firsthand experience and realization that your nightmares won't come true cannot be understated.

- Action can take many forms. It can be as small as smiling at someone or saying hello to them. Next, you might act to shore up your most glaring insecurities, such as your appearance, or that you might sound stupid in front of others. However, these small acts are in preparation for exposure therapy.

- Exposure therapy is a process of facing your fear head-on, but starting from relatively benign instances and graduating incrementally to more anxiety-inducing ones. It is characterized by creating a goal stepladder in which you lay out Point A and Point B—where you are right now, where you want to be, and the path to get there. It can take time, but undoubtedly it will be a slower process than CBT. It functions by exposing you to what you fear, and then making you realize that your emotions are skewing your perception and the world won't end.

- Another way to take action outside of (but inevitably similar to) exposure therapy is to engage in actions similar to what you fear, but in safe situations. These acts include: doing what you fear but in a safe scenario, do something similar to what you fear that brings up the same feelings, and practicing what you fear but in a controlled environment.

- Create an alter ego to make any type of action easier for you. Imagine wearing a mask during Halloween; you feel quite empowered and fearless, don't you? You can translate that same feeling to your daily life if you set about creating an alter ego in an intentional manner, from knowing exactly what their purpose is, what traits they will personify, and all the details that make them whole. This will make it easier to seamlessly slip into, for confident action.

- Identity diversification is making sure that you have multiple different sources of validation, self-esteem, identity, and contentment so that trouble in any one area doesn't completely destabilize you.

- Finally, mindfulness techniques can help us relax the tension that comes with low self-confidence and meet our full experience in the present (including the negative feelings) with calm, curious attention.

Chapter 5. The Confidence Transformation Formula by Dr. Aziz Gazipura

Do you want more confidence? Who doesn't?

Virtually everyone can benefit from more confidence, and undoubtedly that's why you are reading this book. You realize that more confidence doesn't just make you feel better on the inside; it also produces better results on the outside.

The most confident version of you is more socially skilled, well-liked, desired, and sought after. This version of you is also the most effective at solving problems, delivering value, and earning more money in the world. Confidence truly is the Master Skill. And that's why I've been obsessed with it for going on fifteen years now.

It all began one spring day when I finally reached my breaking point at the age of twenty-one. I had spent almost a decade stuck in shyness, social anxiety, and self-loathing. Having no self-confidence was so ingrained it was basically a fixed personality trait in my view. A decade of almost no dates, staying silent in groups, feeling inferior around others, and generally feeling bad about myself as a person.

All this pain and frustration compounded until one day—literally in one moment of one day—I decided that I was going to get this confidence thing handled once and for all.

Actually, to be honest, it wasn't so broadly focused on confidence in life. It was about ladies. I made a decision that I was going to do whatever it took to overcome my fear of women and to learn how to date. I didn't realize it at the time, but what I was really looking for was mastery of my inner confidence... Not just in dating, but in all relationships, my social life, my career, my physical health, and everything else.
Discovering that confidence was a learnable skill that gave me one of the greatest senses of liberation and power I had ever felt in my life. I became obsessed. I read everything I could get my hands on; studied with any teacher I could, and even pursued a doctoral degree in clinical psychology.

As I began to grow and see results, I became very interested in helping others do the same. As I became freer, I wanted to teach others what I had learned so they too could enjoy more self-esteem, relationship and career success, and overall confidence.

There was just one problem.

I didn't exactly know how I had done it. My approach was certainly not systematic, methodical, or strategic. It was more of a frantic binge of taking in information and rapidly applying what I had learned. So what were the elements that actually worked? How had I become so motivated? How did I get myself to take action on the things that scared me, when in the past I used to avoid them like the plague? How did I change my beliefs about myself and reinvent my identity?

These were the questions I began asking, and searching for solutions for. They became part of my obsession. For my focus had grown. It was no longer: "How can I constantly grow and maximize my own confidence in life?" It became: "How can I constantly grow, maximize my confidence *and inspire and teach others to do the same?*"

After all these years, guess what? It turns out there's actually a formula. Like anything, if you do it long enough, you start to see patterns emerge.

I sat down with my journal and dove in: My

goal is to help others produce the transformation I have experienced and continue to experience in my life. This isn't just minor change or slow growth, this is complete transformation—of my identity, how I show up in the world, and what I'm capable of. It's a radical transformation. And it happened fast. It continues to happen, year after year.

Radical means thorough, complete, and total; changing the fundamental nature of something. I hated how much of the talk in my doctoral training was focused on "symptom management of psychopathology." There was such a limited, negative view of the human potential. Genetic determinism was rampant. At best "patients" could hope to "manage" their horribly limiting afflictions.

Forget that. I didn't want to manage social anxiety; I wanted to be liberated from it. I didn't want my coaching or programs to be like vitamin supplements, where you take them and someone asks you, "are they working?" and you say, "hmm. I'm not sure. I think so." That is not radical. I want clients to be astonished by how different their life is now versus how it was years ago. Astonished and grateful. Just like I am whenever I think about where I was then and where I am now.

And rapid? Well who doesn't want to go fast in

this age? I am realistic, however. Because we're talking about changing patterns of thought, emotion, and behavior that have been practiced hundreds of thousands of times over years or decades. So in this case "rapid" does not mean the instant-thirty-second-microwave-popcorn variety. It means changing a pattern of twenty years in twelve months (while noticing big breakthroughs along the way).

Now that I had the target clarified, I had to uncover what created that result. I thought about myself and every client I ever had who was a "rock star". Someone who showed up, dove in, did whatever it took, and really created this R^2 Transformation in their own life. What did they do differently than others? Why were they successful?
I kept asking this question, drawing out graphs, frantically taking notes like a mad scientist searching for the elixir.

After enough digging, I came up with a rough draft of the formula, which I promptly tested by running every client I could think of through it, rating them on each component. Sure enough, the most successful clients scored the highest on all components. The least successful clients had one or more component that was quite low, and they were unable to change this significantly over the course of our work together.

After a few final tweaks, I settled upon the formula that I have seen to accurately predict how to get radical and rapid transformation in your confidence (and ultimately any area of life).

$$R^2 = C \times TO \times 2A \times OMOS$$

Exciting huh? Well, maybe not quite yet because it's unclear what all these random letters mean. But stick with me. Understanding this will help you turn your quest for confidence from a random, partially successful endeavor into the most empowering and rapid growth of your life.

To use this formula, start by thinking of an area of your life you want rapid and radical transformation in. Perhaps it's your confidence, your self-esteem, your dating life and relationships, or your career. This formula works best when you pick a specific area to focus on.

So what is that area for you? Take just a moment to think of one now, so that you can apply this formula as you learn it. This will take it from the realm of abstract theory and turn it into a real experience in your mind and body as you read.

Have one now? Great. Let's dive into the components.

Clarity

First and foremost you need clarity. When I first began my confidence journey I had complete clarity on what I wanted. I wanted to be able to approach women I'm attracted to and actually have a conversation with them. I also wanted to be able to ask them out, go on dates, and eventually have a girlfriend.

Clarity is essential so you know how to direct your focus and energy. It guides you to know exactly what you can do each week, each day, to build your confidence and achieve the result you want.

When I speak with clients, I often find there is a surprising lack of clarity, even though they know they want something to be different. These are the kinds of things they will say:

"I want to feel better."
"I want to be more confident."
"I want a better social life."
"I want to be able to date more."

While none of these is bad, there is one problem. They are all lacking clarity and specificity. Knowing that "I want to be more confident" doesn't really help me know what to do that day to achieve it.

So I help them clarify further by asking something like this: "If you were completely confident in yourself, what would that look like? What would you do?"
They might say, "Well, I would speak up more at work and stop hesitating so much in meetings. I'd stop feeling so anxious around others and start valuing my ideas more."

I want to be more confident becomes:

- Speak up more at work
- Hesitate less (i.e. more immediate action)
- Value my ideas
- Feel less anxious

This is extremely valuable, because now you are able to set some specific targets for the next week or two. If you want to speak up more, you can look for opportunities to do so immediately. You can address the fears you have in that specific situation, mentally challenge them, and then take action in the real world.

All of a sudden your process of personal growth goes from something like this: *I have this big confidence issue to work on* (vague) to something like this: *I'm going to ask a question in the meeting tomorrow* (very specific). How clear can you make your goal? What are the specifics for you?

Total Ownership

In order to produce a rapid and significant change in your life, you must take total ownership of your life. Total ownership means you acknowledge that you are responsible to get where you want to go. You are responsible for the quality of your own life, and no one else is going to take care of that for you.

This need for personal responsibility may sound obvious as you read this, but I am continually amazed at all the subtle ways we can operate as if this were not so. All the little ways we give up responsibility, wanting others, or life, or God to do it for us.

Just the other day I was in the kitchen with my wife and two small children. I'd returned from the gym and was making myself breakfast, chatting with my oldest son. All of a sudden, I hear the loud beep of a truck backing up and instantly remember it's trash day, and I hadn't put the garbage out.

"Did you put the cans out last night?" I asked my wife.

"No." She replied.

I was out in a flash. I ran out to the street to scout out the scene. There the garbage truck was, just passing our house. I grabbed our trash can and moved it to the curb, watching the truck move to the next house.

Then I had this fascinating little moment. My mind said: *Ehh, you tried. Maybe he'll come back later and get it. If not, we'll just deal with it.*

And then I had a counter voice in my head: *Deal with it later? What does that even mean? He's definitely not coming back randomly to check for houses that didn't have their garbage out earlier. If you want to handle it, do it now.*

And so I did. I ran down the street and flagged down the driver. I told him the situation and asked him if I could wheel my can down to his truck so he could put it in. Then I ran back to my house, got the can, and brought it back to him so he could dump it into his truck. I then returned the can to our yard, and walked back into our house, triumphant. Tall and proud, like a beloved king who returns to his home city after many years of frontier wars for conquest and glory.

Where are you giving up your personal responsibility? How are you handing it to others? This pattern can show up in many ways. Here are some of the most common manifestations of a lack of total ownership, which is also known as a victim stance to life:

Waiting for Magic – You aren't taking consistent action towards your goals and dreams. Instead you are waiting for life to somehow get better, as if by magic. Instead of overcoming my fear of approaching and asking women out, for many years I hoped it would "just somehow work out." Perhaps a beautiful, friendly, intelligent woman would move in next door to me, and then we'd start dating. *(Yeah. That never happened.)*

Entitled – Others owe it to you. Your boss should be more relaxed, your spouse should be more understanding, and your friends should reach out to you more. The reason you're not happy is because others are not doing what they should do. If only everyone did exactly what you wanted then you'd feel great and life would go your way. When we're playing this kind of victim-stance game, we feel a lot of blame and frustration toward the people and circumstances in our lives. Our internal mottos are: *It's not fair* and *it's your fault!*

Helpless – *What's the point? I've tried everything and nothing ever worked. I'm doomed to be stuck with _____ forever* (my weight, my lack of social skills, bad job, being single, being stuck in an unhappy relationship, etc.). This pessimistic form of victim-stance drains you of energy and makes you feel utterly powerless. When in a state of helplessness, you predict failure and eventually stop trying to effect change.

Hopeless – If you live in a state of helplessness long enough you will eventually become hopeless. The future looks bleak. Your mind says: I am a victim of circumstance and I can't effect any real change in my life, so I'm destined to live out this unsatisfying existence. Why? Because there's something wrong with me. I'm defective. I'm broken. Oh, and because my parents sucked and so did my school and my teacher in fourth grade. And my boss is a jerk now. And I've tried a bunch of stuff in the past and it didn't work. All that self-help stuff is full of it.

We can go down that last rabbit hole of hopelessness for as long as you like. In fact, you may have spent way more time there, or in one of the other victim stances, than you care to admit. I know I have.

And that's ok. The path to total ownership is an ongoing practice of noticing when we are in victim-land and then consciously reclaiming our power. This doesn't mean discounting that you may have experienced some very painful moments in the past. In fact, taking ownership actually means you take the time to focus on these experiences and actively heal from them.

The attitude of total ownership is characterized by statements like this:
- Yes. I can.
- I will.
- I got this.
- Bring it on.
- I don't know how yet, but I will figure it out.
- I am responsible.
- If I want it bad enough, I can make it happen.

What is an area of your life where you already embody total ownership? Perhaps it's with your health, or finances, or in a particular relationship in your life. Heck, it might even be in a video game! I've talked with clients who get extremely determined and in a state of total ownership when it comes to beating a certain game. They focus their attention, plan their approach, and execute. When they hit obstacles, they find new solutions. When they fail, they learn and try again immediately.

What if they applied that exact same approach to their dating life? Or their health, or finances, or their career?

What if you did? Take a moment now to reflect on the area in your life that you want radical and rapid transformation in. What is it? And what specifically do you want? Do you have clarity? Have you taken the time to reflect and come up with what you want? If not, that in itself may be a sign of a lack of total ownership.

Once you have clarity, ask yourself this question: On a scale of 0-10, how much ownership have I been taking in this area? (0 being none and 10 being complete and total ownership).

Then ask yourself these follow-up questions:
- Why this number? Why not lower?
- What am I doing to make it this high?
- How can I make it even higher?
- What would it look like if I were a 10?

As you ask these questions of yourself, notice what answers emerge. There is no "right" answer. There is no singular path, and your path is not straight. Sometimes total ownership is jacking up the speed and taking more on. Doing more in less time. Sometimes total ownership is slowing down, taking care of yourself, and taking on less!

While the answers may vary, the questions remain the same. Keep asking yourself these questions when you notice a lack of progress in the area you want. Find a way to get yourself to total ownership, and your success becomes inevitable.

Action x 2

Clarity + Total Ownership? You are becoming unstoppable my friend. But there is still one key ingredient missing, and that is action. The people who experience the fastest and biggest changes in their lives take action. Period.

Small action, big action, incremental action, massive action. All of the above. Bold Action is how you will challenge limited stories, break free from the past, create the future you want, and achieve extraordinary results. Action will set you free.

Specifically, there are two kinds of action that are required to transform your confidence in any area of life.

Immediate Action

You must implement what you learn swiftly. The most successful clients I have, apply what they learn after a coaching call the very next day or week. Instead of pondering the implications of possibly, one day taking a risk, ... They just do it.

We talk about their fears of speaking up in a meeting and do a role-play of how they might do it anyway. They're nervous during the role-play. The next day they go to work and they're nervous in the meeting. And yet they speak up anyway. As Scott Allan would say, they "do it scared."

I could give hundreds of specific examples from clients' lives, but the major theme is immediate action. Immediate. As in now. Or tomorrow. Or this week. Not in a few weeks, or next season, or "when things calm down." Right. Now.

We have so much access to inspiring education right now, it's ridiculous. Podcasts on every subject: YouTube videos of brilliant people sharing their wisdom for free, and an endless stream of audiobooks. We can be learning 24-7. And sometimes we confuse this intellectual stimulation with actual growth. But it's not. In fact, the more you do it, the less likely you are to actually apply what you learn because you're spending all your time taking in new information. You're addicted to the titillating excitement of learning something new.

While there's nothing inherently wrong with learning, and I personally love to stimulate my brain, you have to be honest with yourself and see how much you're applying. If you're growing like crazy, and your life is becoming more and more amazing each day then keep studying. But if you "know" all the right solutions, but you still don't like your job, or your spouse, or your body, or something else in your life, then the answer is probably not in another book.

The answer you seek is inside of your very next action. And the one after that. And the one after that... So what action are you going to take... right now?

Consistent Action

Immediate action is essential but not sufficient for total transformation. We've all experienced the flurry and fervor of massive action. The burst of energy, determination, willpower, and excitement when starting something new. And then...where did all my motivation go? Often times, when we don't see immediate results from our immediate action, we get impatient and lose our drive. *I worked out hard for four days in a row and I don't have a six-pack yet?? Well, forget it then.*
I know this sounds silly and absurd, yet it is exactly what we do. We all have an inner three-year-old that wants the treat and wants it NOW.

Consistent action is what sets you up for long term, deep transformation and success. Deep transformation is not just a new behavior, like speaking up in a meeting once, or approaching someone you desire once in a while. It's the fundamental change in your identity that comes from doing something repeatedly hundreds of times.

If you want to become the kind of person who speaks up in groups then consistently speak up in groups. This logic can be applied to literally anything. In fact we could just use it as a formula for identity transformation:

If you want to be the kind of person who does _____, then consistently do ____ starting now.

Yes, even before you're good at it. Even if you might make a mistake (gasp!) or get rejected (double gasp!), or fail (double-mega gasp!).

Stop waiting until you're magically good before you start. Just go now, and keep going. Let it be messy and uncomfortable, because life is messy and uncomfortable. Have you seen wolves kill a bison and then eat the carcass? Have you seen a human baby being born? Messy and uncomfortable indeed.

What about the epitome of transformation—the caterpillar becoming a butterfly? Did you know that inside the cocoon the caterpillar loses all structure and form and turns into a gelatinous mush? This mush then magically reforms into a freaking butterfly. Leaving aside the mind-boggling innate intelligence in this process, let's just look at the caterpillar's experience for a moment. I bet that sure feels messy and uncomfortable for the caterpillar to disintegrate all its flesh into liquid goo.

Speaking up in a meeting doesn't sound so bad now, does it? Or having that conversation you've been avoiding with your husband. Or getting up a bit earlier so you can go to the gym.

The dramatic transformation that you're after won't really show up in a dramatic fashion. Unlike the climax of a movie, you most likely will not vanquish the evil villain, save the company, and rescue the prince/princess all on one epic Saturday evening. Instead transformation looks like you squeezing your hand into a fist, feeling it shake and become sweaty, noticing your heart pounding, taking in a deep breath, and putting your voice forward into the room. It's hearing your alarm go off in the dark and sitting up right away instead of hitting the snooze. Day in and day out. Step by step. Incremental action, consistently applied over time, creates the most extraordinary results.

OMOS

Ok, so let's recap. So far, you have gained a specific clarity about what confidence would look like for you in a key area of your life. You stepped into Total Ownership and are willing to do what it takes to make it happen. And, you are diving in and taking immediate and consistent action.

That might seem sufficient, and it is... to some degree. But the component that ties it all together is OMOS: On My Own Side. That is being on your own side no matter what.
This phrase captures a mixture of self-esteem, self-compassion, and self-love. It means you don't turn on yourself after mistakes, setbacks or failures. You continually find your way back to being encouraging and patient with yourself, even if your progress seems slow, or your desired outcomes are just not quite working out yet.

This is in stark contrast for how most people operate. Instead of being on their own side, they are constantly driving themselves with harsh demands and critical statements. They dismiss their achievements and continually tell themselves a story of inadequacy. And they habitually berate themselves for a million and one things including their performance, appearance, popularity, skills, wealth, and on and on.

Many people use this unpleasant mixture of negative energy as a form of fuel, to drive them forward. The twisted logic goes something like this: *If I continually highlight how much I suck, then I'll be extra super motivated to try harder and achieve faster.*

Not only does this not actually motivate anyone in the long term (from athletes, to children, to employees), it also produces a toxic nest of fear, tension, and low self-esteem inside of you. Which, in turn, robs you of the drive, happiness, and juice to get out there and make stuff happen. Aside from making you feel bad, this lack of self-love actually impairs your results as well. Just imagine this scenario:

A man is about to meet a woman for a date. He met her online and this is their first time together in person. He parks his car outside the agreed upon restaurant. He flips down a mirror in his car and scans his appearance. He notes the bags under his eyes and how they make him look tired. His hair is thinning as well. He already knew that, but every time he sees it, he feels a pang of fear and inferiority.

He steps out of his car and begins walking towards the restaurant, painfully aware that his clothes aren't especially hip or trendy. He happens to see several men standing next to a nearby parked car, casually chatting with each other. They seem so confident, upright, powerful, and loud. He feels another pang of lack and inadequacy, imagining that deep down his date would rather be with a man like that. Now, how does the date go?

Well, who knows? He could just be nervous and insecure beforehand and then find his confidence a bit later in the date. Perhaps all his self-loathing melts and his bold and playful real self emerges. And perhaps not. Quite often this kind of constant self-criticism creates inner fear, tension, and hesitancy, which all lead to poorer outcomes. When tense and hesitant. we are less able to connect, put our ideas out there, be bold, and make in impact at work, in our relationship, or even just out at a party.

I have seen many highly successful clients become very stuck on this component. They are doing everything else right—they have clarity, they're taking total ownership, and they are in constant action. And yet nothing seems to be going their way. They keep getting rejected for jobs or dates. They just can't resolve that issue at work. They are unable to improve things in their relationship.

While they might be doing all the "right" things on the outside, they're not right inside of themselves. They are at odds with themselves and sabotaging their success at every step. You cannot beat yourself into confidence. You cannot verbally abuse yourself into taking action, putting yourself out there, or being bold.

It just won't work in the short or long term. The key to deep transformation is OMOS. The more you are on your own side, the more progress you will make, and the better you will feel about yourself every step of the way.

So, there you have it! The Confidence Transformation Formula. You can use this as you see fit. For some, it's very helpful to give themselves a rating for each component, from 0-10. I often do this with clients to help them pinpoint what they need to grow or change in order to keep making progress.

You'll notice the formula has each component multiplied together, instead of added. This is because each component is essential. If you had complete clarity, were taking total ownership, and fully on your own side, but you were taking absolutely zero action, then your transformation would be zero. Every element matters. Each one is essential.

Any time you feel stuck, return to this formula. You will quickly and easily pinpoint exactly what you need to increase in order to keep moving forward.

Takeaways:

- Dr. Aziz is one smart guy. Throughout his literal decades in the study of confidence, he has developed what amounts to a formula for gaining confidence in every field of life. *$R^2 = C \times TO \times 2A \times OMOS$.*

- Clarity - understand what you want and why.
- Total ownership - take responsibility and don't deflect onto others.
- Immediate and consistent action - you can't just logic yourself into confidence, can you?
- On my own side - be kind and compassionate to yourself, and don't set yourself up for failure.

Summary Guide

CHAPTER 1. THE RIPPLE EFFECT OF CONFIDENCE

- Confidence, or lack thereof, plays an integral role in our everyday lives. You likely don't realize the assumptions you make in either position. You may or may not assume people will like or accept you. You may or may not assume that things will go well. You may or may not believe in yourself.
- These are all unfortunate ways in which our mindsets are skewed. Things are made worse because of the part of human psychology that possesses a negativity bias and wants to panic and protect you. This is known as the fight-or-flight response, and it causes our brains to short circuit by way of the amygdala, and not process things from an objective perspective. It causes our brains to be ruled by fear and terror.
- Social anxiety and low confidence are closely connected, often reinforcing one another. We may feel inferior to others and not equal to the task of putting ourselves

out into the world, fearing rejection or discomfort.

- This is further exacerbated by the spotlight effect, which is when we feel that people are always focusing on us and watching our mistakes, causing massive amounts of anxiety and self-consciousness. In fact, this is just a reflection of our own hypervigilance.

- Low confidence can make us believe that others *cause* us to feel the emotions we do. In reality, we perceive an event, and it's our interpretation of it that results in our emotional response. We are responsible for this middle step. If we become conscious of our own negative interpretations, we can take charge of our emotional landscape.

- The brain, the amygdala in particular, is responsible for this negativity bias and our tendency to act automatically and unconsciously. We need to consistently slow down, become aware, and make our thoughts and feelings conscious.

- One confidence-building technique is to create a Confidence Resume—an objective list of your positive traits and achievements to draw on to counteract negative narratives about yourself.

CHAPTER 2. CORE BELIEFS AND AUTOMATIC THOUGHTS

- Core beliefs are at the root of your lack of confidence. They can manifest in many ways. Typically, they come from a set of automatic thoughts that have been occurring since childhood that you have never analyzed or corrected. Thus, you don't know anything different, or less detrimental, to yourself. This is characterized by faulty assumptions, self-monitoring, and safety behaviors, all of which compound on each other.

- The way to change your patterns of thought is to challenge your core beliefs and automatic thoughts, and this is done through a process called cognitive behavioral therapy, or CBT. CBT is the act of observing your thoughts, and the method we will be talking about is aptly called *cognitive restructuring*. We are all driven by unconscious beliefs and assumptions that influence our actions, and this is a process aimed at making this work for our benefit.

- For our purposes, CBT takes the form of using a thought diary to examine an ACB process: activating event, consequence, and belief. The important part is to understand the belief, because that is what unlocks confidence, or the lack thereof. Then, replace that belief with a more factual, accurate, and empowering one.

- Finally, even though it's healthy and sometimes necessary to speak of what ails us, there is a limit. Anxiety tends to build on anxiety, so when you continue to speak out and ruminate about your worries, you are not seeking catharsis anymore, you are placing yourself into a spiral of negativity and unhappiness. Simply STOP—tell these thoughts to shut up and move on!

CHAPTER 3. COGNITIVE DISTORTIONS

- What is a cognitive distortion? It is a pattern of thinking that is unrepresentative of reality. This is significant because most cognitive distortions are disempowering and cause you to doubt yourself, lose confidence, and lose mental toughness. How can you be mentally tough if the world seems to be pitted against you? You're just starting from a place where you can't win.
- Cognitive distortions are often automatic thought patterns that arise from our own insecurities and fears. They aren't totally unfounded, but they depart wildly from reality. They are characterized by jumping to conclusions based on assumptions and

incomplete information, as well as overreactions.

- A few of the most well-known and dangerous cognitive distortions are all-or-nothing thinking, personalizing, overgeneralizing, catastrophizing, magnifying and minimizing, and jumping to conclusions. An especially notable cognitive distortion that robs us of resilience is emotional reasoning. This is when reality is defined by the emotions we feel at that very moment. Another is perfectionism, which can often lead to us *never* feeling adequate and the phenomenon of imposter syndrome.

- Comparisons are not necessarily a cognitive distortion, but they create the same skewed reality and set of expectations. You should evaluate yourself according to your own baseline, instead of comparing your worst to other people's best.

- Acceptance commitment therapy (ACT) is a simple but powerful approach where we convert our awareness of our own thought patterns into concrete action. We learn to be aware of and accept how we feel, and then we consciously choose the direction we want to take instead according to our values. Finally, we take action, no matter how small, in that direction. We don't *have to* act on negative thoughts and feelings!

CHAPTER 4. THE IMPORTANCE OF ACTION (... AND EXACTLY HOW TO DO IT)

- Sometimes, talk is cheap. At the very least, talking your way to confidence through recognizing cognitive distortions and engaging in cognitive behavioral therapy is a slow and unwieldy process. Action, on the other hand, gets things done a little bit quicker.

- When we think about confidence, we want to feel confident and comfortable before taking action. But that's the wrong way of looking at it and will leave you waiting and searching far longer than you should. Instead, you should understand that action *causes* confidence. The power of firsthand experience and realization that your nightmares won't come true cannot be understated.

- Action can take many forms. It can be as small as smiling at someone or saying hello to them. Next, you might act to shore up your most glaring insecurities, such as your appearance, or that you might sound stupid in front of others. However, these small acts are in preparation for exposure therapy.

- Exposure therapy is a process of facing your fear head-on, but starting from relatively benign instances and graduating incrementally to more anxiety-inducing ones. It is characterized by creating a goal stepladder in which you lay out Point A and Point B—where you are right now, where you want to be, and the path to get there. It can take time, but undoubtedly it will be a slower process than CBT. It functions by exposing you to what you fear, and then making you realize that your emotions are skewing your perception and the world won't end.

- Another way to take action outside of (but inevitably similar to) exposure therapy is to engage in actions similar to what you fear, but in safe situations. These acts include: doing what you fear but in a safe scenario, do something similar to what you fear that brings up the same feelings, and practicing what you fear but in a controlled environment.

- Create an alter ego to make any type of action easier for you. Imagine wearing a mask during Halloween; you feel quite empowered and fearless, don't you? You can translate that same feeling to your daily life if you set about creating an alter ego in an intentional manner, from knowing exactly what their purpose is, what traits they will personify, and all the details that make them whole. This will make it easier to seamlessly slip into, for confident action.

- Identity diversification is making sure that you have multiple different sources of validation, self-esteem, identity, and contentment so that trouble in any one area doesn't completely destabilize you.

- Finally, mindfulness techniques can help us relax the tension that comes with low self-confidence and meet our full experience in the present (including the negative feelings) with calm, curious attention.

CHAPTER 5. THE CONFIDENCE TRANSFORMATION FORMULA BY DR. AZIZ GAZIPURA

- Dr. Aziz is one smart guy. Throughout his literal decades in the study of confidence, he has developed what amounts to a formula for gaining confidence in every field of life. $R^2 = C \times TO \times 2A \times OMOS.$
- Clarity - understand what you want and why.
- Total ownership - take responsibility and don't deflect onto others.
- Immediate and consistent action - you can't just logic yourself into confidence, can you?

- On my own side - be kind and compassionate to yourself, and don't set yourself up for failure.

www.ingramcontent.com/pod-product-compliance
Lightning Source LLC
Chambersburg PA
CBHW070644150426
42811CB00051B/540